DAVID&SON

Mudgett, Avram, and Ethan Davidson
Amecameca, DF, Mexico, 1963

Photo by Grania Davidson Davis

DAVID&SON

Peregrine Parentus and Other Tales

Avram Davidson
&
Ethan Davidson

Edited by

Grania Davidson Davis

Surinam Turtle Press
RAMBLE HOUSE
2016

First hardcover edition

Surinam Turtle Press
an imprint of
Ramble House
10329 Sheephead Drive
Vancleave MS 39565 USA

ISBN 13: 978-1-60543-894-8

SOURCES

'Sambo' by Avram Davidson & Ethan Davidson
Eidolon, Volume 6, Number 1, Autumn 1996, Australia

'Avram Davidson' © Carol Carr
Everybody Has Somebody in Heaven: Essential Jewish Tales of the Spirit
by Avram Davidson, edited by Jack Dann and Grania Davidson Davis
Devora Publishing, 2000
Carol Carr: The Collected Writings, by Carol Carr
Surinam Turtle Press, Ramble House, 2014

'Arnten of Ultima Thule' by Avram Davidson
Worlds of IF Science Fiction, July-August 1971

Surinam Turtle Press #60

DAVID&SON

TABLE OF CONTENTS

~.~.~.~.~

Introduction

Avram and Ethan, a Love Story

Grania Davidson Davis

SOMEONE ONCE ASKED me who was the love of Avram Davidson's life. Without hesitation I replied, "Ethan."

After Ethan was born in 1962, Avram described the experience in the Seattle fanzine, 'Cry of the Readers.'

SON OF CRY OF THE READERS

Dear CRYptonymous Readers & Staff:
   You all know, I'm sure, how, about three weeks after our marriage, I was informed by one wife, two MDs, and two frogs (madly laying eggs), that I was destined to become a father in about one week and eight months, and—what? No, dammit, not of the tadpoles!—etc. The date of the Grand Opening, as my mother-in-law called it, was first set for Nov. 13. It was then moved to Nov. 16. It was next moved to Nov. 11. I set my face like flint agin any earlier date, inasmuch on Nov. 11 we would have been married nine months (in fact, on Nov. 11, we *were* married nine months!). All things considered, Nov. 11th seemed like a very appropriate day for Embryo Homunculus Davidson to make his or her 1st public appearance. True, from time to time during the latter part of October, Grania would remark, pensively, that "Hallowe'en would make a nice birthday, don't you think?" "Not in *my* religion," I assured her. . . .

The weekend of the 11th friends came to guest with us. Grania announced that she intended to go into labor at 10 P.M. the night of the 10th. The baby could be born about 4 A.M. and we could all sleep late on Sunday. We commended her for her thoughtfulness, packed her bag for the hospital, and waited. Ten P.M. came, ten p.m. went, completely unnoticed by the mother-elect, who was deep in an animated account of how she lost a job as bar-maid in New Orleans because she did not know how to dice with the customers for the juke-box: a quaint local custom of the Belle Ville of March Gras, Spanish Moss, Red-Beans-And-Rice.

Eleven P.M. came. Still no labor. "Maybe you should take a hot bath?" I suggested. "Or go horse-back riding." "I know what I'll do," she said, brightly; "I'll do deep knee-bends." She did knee-bends for 20 minutes. All she got was stiff knees. At three A.M. we stopped waiting and at 5 A.M. we went to bed (except for Mr. Guest who, described by his lady as "The national free-style sleeping champion," had gone some hours ego.) Next afternoon Mrs. Guest made blintzes for us. Good, too. "As soon as I finish eating my cheese-blintzes," Grania assured us, "I'm going to go into labor." Our guests left at midnite, labor not yet having started.

So much for Nov. 11th. I felt I'd lost all faith in my child. My mother had a Mystical Vision that Grania would turn her into a—no, not a pumpkin; a grandmother . . .

All this, I understand, is about par for the course— "false labor" and lateness are both quite common in first parturitions. But by Monday I felt as if I were pregnant myself, and by Tuesday I was ready to engage in the *couvade*—a curious tribal custom of the Amazon or Guiana or Bongo-Bongo Land, whereby the *husband* goes into labor! He groans in his hammock and the neighbor-men come and wipe his face with a cold towel and say Push Down, Joe, and There There Sam it's going to be All Right, you'll see; and, Say, Bert, you remember you had the same thing when you gave birth to Sylvester . . . the *wife*, meanwhile, is out back behind a banana bush having the baby without any fuss whatsoever. We may laugh at these simple savages, but after all, they are Close to Nature, and who knows? Eh?

~ ~ ~ ~ ~

So much for November 12-25...

~ ~ ~ ~ ~

Eight pounds, six ounces. Twenty-one inches long . . . I filled out the name-form. ETHAN MICHAEL ANDERS DAVIDSON, *Male*. He certainly was male. Besides having the normal male appurtenances, he had a rugged face and broad hands. Didn't look like anyone in particular—just looked Jewish. Boy, did he ever! It was night when I finally left the hospital; not night still—but night *again*. The stars were even brighter, and I had the primal instinct to shout—as I'm sure all new fathers of sons have had since Adam—"I have a son! Me! My son! Hey, listen, everybody, listen: My son, the baby! Wheee! Gosh! Et sickeningly cetera . . . ."

So there you are. Exit, Embryo Homunculus. Enter, Ethan Michael Anders.

~ ~ ~ ~ ~

Avram and I were married in February, 1962, in Damon Knight's stately mansion in Milford, Pennsylvania. Chasidim danced, and Theodore Sturgeon played guitar. Nine months and change later, our son Ethan Davidson was born in Manhattan, where we lived at that time. A series of adventures and misadventures took us to Amecameca DF, Mexico, between two giant volcanoes. There Avram and I separated, and we all moved to the San Francisco Bay Area. The marriage didn't continue, but the relationship did, focused around Ethan.

Later, in 1968, I married Dr. Stephen Davis, and we became an extended family. We moved around a bit, from California to Hawaii, and Avram usually tried to be nearby. Late one night Ethan had a serious health crisis. While we tried to deal with it, there was a knock on the door. Who could it be at that hour? It was Avram, who said he dropped by to surprise us. We were surprised indeed.

After Ethan grew up, Avram moved to Washington State. Now Ethan commuted to visit his father, as Avram grew older and sicker, and finally passed away in 1993. Ethan describes the later part of Avram's life in his introduction to this book, "Avram's Last Years."

(I described more about life with Avram in the introductory Memoir to my story collection *Tree of Life, Book of Death: The Treasures of Grania Davis,* Ramble House, 2013.)

Avram's love for Ethan likely inspired this excerpt from *The Boss in the Wall* (by Avram Davidson and Grania Davis, Tachyon, 1998, short-listed for the Nebula Award):

"She has her ways, what child has not? And the mere way she has of standing in a doorway with a wry, dry look on her small face makes her parents wonder how the doorway ever existed before she came to stand in it."

The tales in this book also have their own history. We designed *David&Son* to resemble an old 'Ace Double.' Half of the book is a classic, never reprinted, Avram Davidson fantasy novella *Arnten of Ultima Thule,* first published in 'Worlds of If' in 1971. The other half of the book are the collaborative works of Avram Davidson and Ethan Davidson, one published and the others not.

Peregrine Parentus and 'Pygmies and Cranes' were completed by Ethan from Avram's notes after he passed away. *Peregrine Parentus* is based on Avram's notes for a long-awaited third *Peregrine* novel. 'Pygmies and Cranes' came from Avram's notes for the final *AdVentures in UnHistory* tale.

'The Safety of a Larger Herd' and 'Sambo' are true collaborations, written before Avram's death. 'Sambo' was published in the Australian magazine *Eidolon* in 1996.

'Avram's Last Years' and the delightful 'Avramisms' were written solely by Ethan for *David&Son.* 'The Beach at Rosarito,' written solely by Avram, and based on an incident from Ethan's early childhood, is one of Avram's unpublished *AdVentures in AutoBiography.*

The Afterword 'Avram Davidson' by Carol Carr is, of course, by the inimitable Carol Carr.

I have a number of people to thank for this book: Richard A. Lupoff, who first developed the project for Surinam Turtle Press, and Gavin L. O'Keefe, editor and talented cover artist, who brought it to publication by Fender Tucker's Ramble House. I want to thank Ian Harris for ongoing tech support, and Gordon Eklund for scanning the piece from CRY. I especially want to thank Mark Fuller Dillon, who sent us the PDFs for *Arnten* and much more. And I want to thank the intrepid readers who might happen upon this little book.

Grania Davidson Davis

AVRAM'S LAST YEARS:
AVRAM DAVIDSON — THE VIEW FROM BELOW

Ethan Davidson

MANY PEOPLE HAVE asked me what it was like having Avram as my father. There is no cocktail party answer for this. For one thing, I have no basis of comparison. For another, parent child relationships are always complicated. Finally, he was forty when I was born, forty-four when I was first cognizant, so I missed the majority of his life.

I think the best way to answer that question is in the way that Avram always admonished the creative writing group he once taught in my Other Parents' (My mother and stepfather, that is) living room. Whenever somebody showed up saying they had thought of a great idea for a story, he would kill the impending monolog in the egg by saying "Don't tell it. Write it."

When I was three, my mother and father divorced. They remained good friends, and Avram tried to live near me during most of my childhood. For not being forced to choose, I was and remain grateful to all three parents.

Avram liked to tell me a story from the trip he took across Mexico when I was a toddler. It was the early sixties, he had a beard, and, much to his annoyance, people repeatedly called him "Castro."

One day he went into a shop where the teenage girl behind the counter called him "Castro."

"Why do you call me Castro?" he asked, in Spanish.

"Because you are bearded."

"Then why did you not also mention—and he named several former presidents of Mexico who had beards.

The girl was disinclined to taunt him further.

15

When I was four, I lived with Avram in the Haight Ash-bury with his mother. It was 1966, and his mother was always complaining about people sitting around and not working.

"Behavior," he later said, "that now we might be happy to settle for."

When I was still four, Avram and my mother, Grania, moved to Belize, formerly British Honduras. As usual, they lived apart, but close together. Avram rented a house near Stann Creek, with a large cage on the porch, in which was a "quash." A raccoon like animal with a long nose about the size of a retriever, or so I recall it.

Later, he tried to own a wild bird, but it pecked the cage until it died. He swore to never again try to keep a wild animal as a pet.

I soon moved with my mother to Gales Point, a remote village reached, generally, only by a long ride on a private boat. But there was a rough dirt road leading to—somewhere.

Avram was still in Stann Creek when he heard on Radio Belize, the only form of mass media there at the time, that a hurricane watch was expected. Somehow he got to wherever the road led, rented a land rover and driver (he himself could not drive), got us, and took us out of harm's way.

Why was he in British Honduras? He had discovered it by accident, an English speaking nation on the other side of Mexico, and got the idea of starting a shipping business.

Why a shipping business in a remote developing nation rather than a grocery store in San Francisco? Because that was the way his mind turned.

So Avram, who had a little experience in agriculture in Israel, and had taken agriculture classes near Los Angeles, but had never tried it in the tropics, decided to buy a plantation, up a remote river reachable only by private boat from a town reachable only by ferry. It seemed simple. The land was available very cheaply so long as you paid a government inspector to inspect it and then testify that it was developed.

He bought it, but never got it inspected. He left. He sent money for maintenance to locals, who spent it on themselves. When I was fourteen he sent me there to see how the land was doing. I spent a year, had a wonderful time, but had to report that the land had fallen to ruins. Only a few fruit trees remained, because fruit thieves had cut the vegetation around them. He sent money to have it cleared. I paid an eccentric Englishman, who lived next door, to hire a team of Mayan Indians to clear it. This was done. I left. I returned at the age of thirty, and was told the neighbor had said the Mayans could stay if they liked. They liked. By the time I returned, there was a small Mayan village. Bare breasted women, naked children, and large turkeys walked around without shame. A small dock had been built, and a charity had installed a tank for pure water.

And this is how I accidentally founded a Mayan village at the age of fifteen.

During most of my childhood, I lived with my mother and stepfather, Steve Davis, in Sausalito, a town near San Francisco, during the week, and spent the weekends with Avram somewhere nearby. Where "nearby" was varied. A lot. I had the habit of moving every six months. So I got to experience quite a variety of towns in the San Francisco Bay area, and quite a variety of housemates, too. Hippies and eccentrics of all sorts seemed comfortable around him, the younger hippies perhaps seeing him as a sort of father figure, who was cool because he had a long beard, long hair, and never wore a suit or tie. His only flaw was his persistent refusal, after a few tries, to smoke marijuana. He much preferred whisky.

When I was eleven, he lived in a place in Mill Valley he called "the flea circus." With its revolving cast of countercultural characters, I can see why. Among the residents was a cocaine dealer and a heroin addict. He told me that the coke dealer had said, "Get out of here you junky, we don't want no junkies around here."

"As if he has the right," he added, "when he is dealing coke."

"But why did he talk to him like that?" I asked.

"At every time there are people whom it is OK to hate. Right now, heroin addicts are the people that it is OK to hate."

When he lived again in San Francisco, in the early seventies when homeless people were not yet covering San Francisco's sidewalks, he spotted one who slept standing up. He invited him to stay over for a while. Even when offered a bed, he preferred to sleep in a chair, saying "sitting down makes you old."

I could see why Avram privately called him "Odd John." Never to his face.

"Where is my five hundred dollars?" He asked one morning.

"I don't know," said Avram.

"OK, fine, I guess you are five hundred dollars richer, that's all."

"I don't have five cents of yours," said Avram, and then: "Here it is."

"God bless you. God bless your soul." said John. "Without that money I would have been in the devil's hands."

And off he went again.

One of my earliest memories is of Avram saying a Jewish prayer over me. He said: "May Gabriel guard the front of you, Michael guard the back of you, Ariel guard your left side, and Rafael guard your right side."

It was very comforting to be surrounded by angels in this way. The sense of being in the middle of a circle surrounded by divine protective entities has returned to me at various times in my life.

But that is the only memory I have of his decades as an ultra Orthodox Jew. The story I heard was that he was in the hospital awaiting surgery, and had called the local Rabbi in. The Rabbi came in smoking a cigar and saying "isn't science wonderful."

He left Avram choking on cigar smoke.

Then Mr. Niwa, a Tenrikyo minister came in and prayed for him by laying hands on him. He said that he felt prayed for.

He converted to Tenrikyo and maintained a life long friendship with Mr. Niwa, a gentle, soft-spoken man.

Many people call Tenrikyo a Shinto sect, but that is not really true. It is a syncretism sect, combining aspects of Shinto, Buddhism and (though they never say so) Christianity.

Its rituals are very Shinto-like in style, but they believe in Karma and reincarnation.

They are also monotheists who worship "God the Parent." The It was started in the nineteenth century by a female prophet.

The daily rituals are a combination of chants and hand movements, both reminding the believers to regularly "sweep away the dust" from their minds.

Sometimes, when Avram said something he regretted having said, he would quickly add "sweep away the dust."

In the early seventies, California was full of young people without the slightest idea of what to do with their lives, and cults were devouring them. In San Francisco, Avram met a woman of this type, and, after talking to her for a while, took her to the nearby home of Mr. Niwa. Although Tenrikyo does seek converts, Mr. Niwa also listened to her for a bit and then told her that this was not a good time for her to be focusing on religion. She needed to work on her own life first.

Avram had served as a medic in World War Two. He had patched up broken soldiers in the caves of Okinawa. He refused to ever let his writing be translated into German, even when he was dead broke and it paid well. But Avram, in the second half of his life, took me to Japan on a religious pilgrimage, and made many Japanese friends.

He attained some sort of clerical position, and, when I married a Japanese woman (no, it did not last), he and Mr. Niwa conducted the ceremony together. He even attempted missionary work. When he briefly taught creative writing in a college in Virginia, he put up flyers inviting students to Tenrikyo services he conducted. He saved one of those flyers, and wrote on it: "Few came, none came twice."

He later wrote to Mr. Niwa that "I am not a missionary. Not everybody is meant to be one."

In his final years, as he saw his life drawing to a close, he gave up pork again. When I asked him why, he said: "I don't have to explain why." In his will, he requested a military headstone in a navy cemetery, with a star of David on it. Avram once told me: "We must choose between a self-created universe and a self-created God."

When I was thirteen, Avram's mother died, and his own health started to fail. I was full of teenage pain. This was not a happy time for us. He moved later to Washington State. He wound up spending three years in a veterans' home, mostly for the free food and shelter. Then he moved to the Navy town of Bremerton. In my twenties, I went to see him there many times. Now he walked with difficulty and mostly used a wheel chair, due to a series of strokes. His apartment was damp in the winter and hard to get in and out of without good working legs. But it was close to the children, who would play in and around his apartment, which he liked. One neighborhood boy, age about seven, wrote him a note saying: "You are my best friend did you no that. I love you did you no that." He saved it, and wrote on it: "Am very moved by the note."

The last visit came. Avram was in the hospital, in a coma. I dropped my plans and flew to Seattle, then took the ferry to Bremerton.

He woke up out of his deep sleep not knowing where he was, saw me, and said:

"Ethan, be a good boy and get me something to read."

I looked around the barren empty hospital room and said: "There is nothing in this room to read."

I could see his mind working, trying to solve a very difficult puzzle, and then he said, slowly: "You mean in this whole room there isn't a single thing to read?"

I affirmed this.

I returned the next day, and, somebody had brought a James Thurber book and some newspapers. They looked well read.

Avram had once told me that although he did drink regularly, he considered reading to be his real vice.

Avram usually slept on one side of his bed, and the other side was covered with books and papers. He once pointed to that pile, the approximate length of a human being, and said: "This is called the writer's mistress."

Avram gave me my first manual typewriter (now they sell them in antique shops), my first electric typewriter, and my first word processor.

The latter was given to him when he was living in the Veterans' Home near Bremerton. It was in a town called Retsil. This is Lister spelled backwards, and there is a story behind that, which I have forgotten. There was nothing in the town but the Veterans' home, a few half-finished looking houses that were presumably inhabited by employees, and a tavern that served beer and wine. The latter was popular with veterans who were in the home due to alcoholism. Avram sometimes went there for a glass of wine.

One reached the town by taking a "Mosquito ferry" from Bremerton to Retsil, then walking up the hill. The staff was complaining that Avram typed late into the night, so he requested something that would function as a typewriter, but make no noise. So, somebody gave him the word processor. Which he later gave to me, completely unused.

"All I want," he said, "is something that types without making noise. But people keep saying 'Let me just show you one more thing.' "

He paused, then said: "Theirs is the spirit that made America great, not mine."

Avram never set foot in cyberspace.

During his last years, Avram did repeat himself a bit, but that just meant that he could get more mileage out of the same joke. More than once he told me that farmers were reporting that modern farming yielded bigger chickens, but they laid fewer eggs.

To which I more than once replied: "I suppose we have to choose which comes first, the chicken or the eggs."

The inevitable call came. Avram had passed. I flew to his place to sort through his stuff.

Avram had once said that he was "living proof that a rolling stone can gather moss." As I went through his boxes, I learned the truth of this. He saved everything, boxes and boxes of stuff, and I had not yet been taught how to figure out what was important. I spent days in these boxes, before friends arrived to help. In a plastic wastebasket, I found an empty pint of vodka, a shopping list, and—the entire manuscript of an unpublished novel.

He had written notes on everything he touched, going so far as to correct his own dictionary.

But my biggest surprise came when I visited the nursing home where he had died.

Among his few possessions there were several letters that he had written, stamped and addressed, literally the day he died.

I read them, put them back, sealed them and put them in a mailbox. Friends who received them talked about how he kept writing them letters from beyond the grave.

There are twenty-six years more of stuff I could say. But instead, I will close with a selection of what I call "Avramisms": phrases he repeated over and over, when the occasion seemed to call for them.

~ ~ ~ ~ ~

AVRAMISMS

Ethan Davidson

AVRAM ENJOYED TELLING jokes, anecdotes, and aphorisms, many of which he made up himself, and some of which he told repeatedly. Often, they were linked to certain activities or situations. A certain thing would trigger him to make a certain remark. Growing up with this, these sayings became part of my mental landscape. So I've decided to type some of them up and put them in this book. I call them Avramisms.

1: Avram told me that he is one third Litvak (Latvian Jew) and thus is very stubborn. But I, Ethan Davidson, am two thirds Litvak, and thus twice as stubborn as he is.

2: Avram said that the thigh is the best part of the chicken. The breast is too rich, the lower leg and wings are too bony, but the thigh is juuust right.

3: Avram told the story of a man who lived with him in the Retsil, Washington veterans home.

   The Social Worker came to visit, and heard Dave say: "Take a s—."

   The Social Worker said: "Now Dave, that's not necessary."

   Dave looked at him with a very puzzled expression and said: "Not necessary to take a s—?"

   (Avram always laughed when he told that story. Sometimes before he even finished telling it.)

4: Avram said: "I grew up around Jews, and learned that when you are nervous, you eat something. Later I learned that the gentiles say, when you are nervous, you drink something. So I started doing both."

5:   Avram never learned to drive, but he did try. When living in British Honduras (now Belize) in the sixties, he observed that the one road in the area seldom had anybody on it, so he decided that this was a good time to learn to drive. He was taking a supervised drive with a friend when a large tapir jumped out in front of them, and his friend had to slam the brakes. He decided that he was not meant to drive and said that "he had tapered off of driving."

6:   Even after he stopped being religiously Jewish (mostly) he still liked to quote 11th century Jewish theologian Moses Maimonede's short review of the New Testament.

"It contains a lot of new things, and a lot of true things. But the new things aren't true, and the true things aren't new."

7:   Avram liked to tell this story from the old country:

A shnorer (mooch) dropped in on a family at dinner time. The meal included both brown bread, known as "bread," and fairly cheap, and challah, a luxury item for this family.

The shnorer began to eat the challah, stuffing a large chunk into his mouth. When he reached for a second, the father said: "Would you like some bread?"

"No thank you," said the shnorer, stuffing a second chunk into his mouth, "I'll just have some more challah."

When he reached for the challah a third time, the father said, more loudly: "Are you sure you wouldn't like some bread?" The shnorer said: "No, challah is fine."

As the shnorer's hands moved towards the last chunk, the father said, "Did you know that this challah costs one whole ruble a loaf?"

"Really?" said the shnorer. "One whole ruble a loaf? Well," and he stuffed the last chunk in his mouth, "it was worth it."

8: Avram told me: "It is because of the Great Wall of China that Rome fell."

"Why?" I asked.

"Because of the great wall," he said, "tribes which otherwise would have pushed east pushed west, displacing other tribes, which pushed west, displacing other tribes, and so on, until, hundreds of years later, it led to the invasion of Rome."

9: If I started a sentence with "If we had—," Avram would often say: "If we had steak, we could have steak and eggs, if we had eggs."

10: When Avram got older, he tended to repeat himself, but this enabled him to get more mileage out of the same joke. More than once he said: "The farmers are saying that the new methods of farming are making the chickens bigger, but they don't lay as many eggs."

And more than once I replied: "I suppose we have to decide which comes first, the chicken or the eggs."

11: When Avram wanted to throw out a random fact, he would say: "Bismarck is the capitol of North Dakota." This became a running joke between us, so much so that when, at age 11, he took me on a Greyhound trip across the USA, we went hundreds of miles out of our way to see Bismarck, North Dakota. When we arrived, there didn't seem to be much to see. We looked at the Capitol building, then took the next bus out.

12: Though Avram, so far as I know, was never an atheist or an agnostic, he did ponder the paradoxes inherent to both religion and science. He summed them up by saying:

"We are forced to choose between a self-created universe and a self-created God."

13: Often, if you called Avram, he would pick up the phone and say, "Ever-ready home baked bagels."

14: When planning things or dealing with hassles, Avram sometimes said: "Everything takes longer than you think it will, everything is more trouble than you think it will be, everything costs more than you think it will."

15: When talking about something complicated, Avram often said: "Things are seldom simple, and this isn't one of them."

16: When Avram ate a piece of fruit, he would often say: "helps fight the dreaded scurvy."

17: When the topic of his health came up, Avram often said: "The only thing more boring than someone else's diet is someone else's disease."

18: Avram's (Japanese) Tenrikyo faith taught him that "Dust" (bad thoughts) tend to settle on our minds. The prayers they chant include the line, "Sweep away the dust." Avram translated the prayers that Tenrikyo members say daily into English, and when he joined in, he alternated between the English and Japanese version, if it was a small gathering of people he knew. And when he said something that he felt reflected bad thoughts, he would often reprimand himself by saying, "Sweep away the dust."

19: When Avram was cooking, he very, very often said: "You can put salt in, but you can't take salt out."

20: Avram probably didn't coin this joke, and I suspect that it goes way back.

Q: What has four legs, fur, and chases cats.
A: Mrs. Cats and her lawyer.
(I know "Mrs. Cats" is spelled Katz. It's meant to be told.)

21: Sometimes when surprised, Avram said, "Well I snum."

22: Avram ate a lot of exotic food, but he also talked about a food that did not exist: Crottled Greeps. He once mentioned that someone's profession was "Greep Crottler," adding, "Well somebody's got to do it."

23: Avram liked to tell this supposedly true story, though when it took place, I don't know.

A businessman in the USA started to do business with the king of Turkey. The king of Turkey came to like him, even visiting him in the USA. One day, he brought Turkey's greatest treasure, a copy of every book every published in Turkey, handsomely bound in leather, and all written in Turkish, which the businessman could not read.

His house was big, but not so big that this white elephant of a gift did not get in the way. He pondered on how to get rid of it without offending His Majesty, and it came to him.

He wrote to the king and said, "Thank you so much for this wonderful gift. But I cannot keep this all to myself. I am donating the full collection to the Library of Congress in Washington DC, so that all of the American people can have access to your nation's great works of fiction, poetry, philosophy, and so forth." And he shipped all the books to the Library of Congress, where, to this day, they remain in some dark shelf in the basement, waiting for anybody who wished to see them.

He sat, satisfied at a job well done. But a few weeks later, the doorbell rang, and he was given a letter and a large stack of boxes whose dimensions and packing materials he had seen before. He opened the letter and read it.

"My dear friend, clearly you are a very generous man. And your generosity should be rewarded. So I have had another copy made of every book ever published in Turkey, bound in high quality leather."

He sighed, and hired somebody to build him more shelves, open the boxes, and put them on the shelves, though in what order he had no idea. And there they sat for the rest of his life, in case the king of Turkey should happen to drop by.

24: Avram told me that he had read that (right wing televangelist) Jerry Falwell had stated that the words: "Separation of church and state" were not in the US constitution. Instead, they were just in the private letters of Thomas Jefferson.

"Nevertheless," said Avram, "I think that most Americans would prefer Thomas Jefferson, with all his vices, to Jerry Falwell, with all his virtues."

25: Avram taught creative writing, for a time, in Grania Davis' living room. Whenever somebody came in saying, "I have a great idea for a story," he would say: "Don't tell it. Write it."

Like many writers, he believed that one should never talk about a work in progress. Yet at parties, he would often be annoyed (he said) by people who asked him: "So, what have you been writing lately."

The only thing he found more annoying were people who came up to him and said: "Say, I have a great idea for a story. How about if I tell it to you, you write it, and we'll split the payment? I'd do it myself if I had the time."

26: When Avram went to the bathroom, he first sometimes said: "Even kings and queens must live by nature."

27: Avram said he once went to a dinner party at a restaurant with several people, including my younger brother Seth Davis, then a small boy. At one point, Seth blurted out: "This mustard is rotten." One of the adults at the table scolded him at length about what a rude and inappropriate thing that was to say in front of company. Meanwhile, one of the other adults said, "This mustard is rotten."

28: Avram told a story from the old country about a shnorer (in this context meaning "begger") who said: "If I was as rich as Rothschild, I'd be *richer* than Rothschild, because I would still shnore a little on the side."

29: When somebody said to Avram, "Nice to see you," he would generally reply: "Nice to be seen."

30: When a disagreement arose regarding a matter of taste, he would usually say: "With taste and scent, no argument."

31: When I was a young boy, he asked me the following riddle:
    Q: "Have you heard about the 3 holes in the ground?"
    A: "No."
    "Well, well, well."

32: When Avram expressed conflicting opinions he would say, "I am large, I contain multitudes."

33: When saying goodbye to somebody, he would often say: "Walk the path of beauty, as the Navajo say."

(I later spent a month on a Navajo reservation, and learned that the "Beauty Path" is an important part of Navajo spirituality.)

"Walk the path of beauty," as Avram would say.

~ ~ ~ ~ ~

THE BEACH AT ROSARITO

Avram Davidson

WHEN THE BOY was born, we said lightheartedly that for his
first haircut all three of us would make the pilgrimage to the
Festival of Simeon bar Jochai at Merom, in Galillee. He is
the Jewish saint who is supposed to have written The Zohar
of the Caballa during thirteen years which he spent in a cave,
secluded from the Hadrianic persecutions. The festa is
unique, it's not celebrated elsewhere, there are dancings and
bonfires, and little boys get their first haircuts. But this is
when they are three years old, and the marriage didn't last
that long—and the religious faith barely.

Somehow, though, as part of the marriage settlement, the
pilgrimage was transmuted into a trip abroad for his mother;
she had never been. We agreed that the little boy should stay
with me this while, and, as we didn't want him to feel aban-
doned by her, we told him (and made it true) that we were all
going on trips—she to Europe, he and I to . . . to . . .

We finally settled on Baja California, and off she went.
Her excited picture postcard accounts came to us for months:
how she had bought him a small reindeer hide at a fjord in
Lapland, how she decided to skip Turkey because of an
alarm about cholera, how all the youth hostels would starve
to death if there were another potato famine. While she was
still counting silos from the train windows en route to New
York, we flew to San Diego, and a quasi-Mexican friend
drove us into Baja, to Rosarito Beach between TJ and Ense-
nada, and where urban sprawl seemed somehow less ugly.
Terms were arranged at a sort of green stucco motel in between the highway and the beach. The friend showed us
what buses to take back for San Diego and drove off, and

there we were, all two of us, with clean clothes for a week. I was forty-two, he was not yet three.

The motel was half-empty, the dueños lived opposite us, in a crazy little house, and they had a fat parrot who strolled around like a chicken, muttering to himself. We had two big rooms and of course the doors didn't close properly. Sand and breezes all over the place. Nobody cared if the little boy wore clothes or not. The beach was broad and nice and there were craggy islands off shore, full of sea birds, and the waves washed in straight from Japan. Horses galloped and trotted up and down. Poseidon. Salt-spray and woodsmoke.

We all live in worlds which are at least half-myth. With children it's more than half. Poseidon wasn't yet in his. The green horses of the sea crashed and broke and rolled up gently. And, gently, we'd go in, with him jumping up and down, babbling with joyful fear as the weak waves washed around his waist. An inhabited station wagon was parked a ways up, and bearded-looking figures lolled in and out of it. Farther on, Mexican women arranged a cook-out and their men played guitars and rollicked songs, all of which really did sound like ¡Hey O Rancho grande!

"George Dupree!" the little boy shouted. I didn't know what he meant. "Here comes another George Dupree!" and he disentangled a long strand of bulbous seaweed from around his minichest. It was new to him, but he had a word for it, straight out of A.A. Milne. It took me a long time to figure it out, but it suddenly came clear. James James Morrison Morrison Weatherbee George Dupree (you may remember) used to say to his mother,

> " Mother," he said, said he: "You must never go down
> to the end of the town, if you go don't down with
> me." *

Back at the ranch was a water hose to wash sand and salt off small boys. The dueños had a young visiting grandson. He slept in the bath tub. There was no plumbing in the crazy

---

* "Disobedience," A. A. Milne, *When We Were Very Young* (1924).

little house. By and by a family arrived with two sons called (and called and called) Candelarito and Rubenito. Mine recognized them at once. "There's Kanga and Roo," he said. And trotted out to play with them. Washed and changed and tingling, we walked dunes and arroyos past a house whose outer walls were covered with flowering potted plants and singing cage-birds. At the little roadside restaurant I eventually ate my way through the menu. He sampled, but mostly he lived on milk and orange juice and refrescos, all with faraway little grunts of pleasure.

The people from the inhabited station wagon were not all bearded. Cats (as they then still were) and chicks went slowly along the beach gathering mussels. Then they made a fire and cooked. One of them, with blond Chester A. Arthur facehair, strolled over. "Do you live in California? In San Francisco, right?" "Yes. I think I've seen you." He squatted down companionably and he told us partly that his name was Shob, and then he and the boy had a conversation, as it might have been between equals. I hardly knew, somehow, which seemed more sweet and harmless. Salt-spray and woodsmoke and horses. Poseidon. Sea birds rising in a cloud from the rocky crag, echo of sea-shriek, great red sun slowly smoldering its way down into the ocean.

Perhaps a year or almost two years later, somebody said that Shob had sold him a cap of acid. Somebody said that the acid was bad. Somebody said the acid had given him a really bad trip. Somebody stabbed Shob twelve times and cut off his right arm and dumped him and his arm, in a gulley somewhere near San Francisco. Shob had gone down to the end of the town, all the way down, and he didn't come back.

But by that time the little boy had forgotten that he had ever known him and he had forgotten the parrot who strolled and the horses and the waves and the sand and the sand dollars and seaweed and the sea birds and star fish, and he thought that Kanga and Roo and George Dupree were familiar to him only from books.

~ ~ ~ ~ ~

PEREGRINE PARENTUS

Avram Davidson & Ethan Davidson

I

GEORGE SPIZZERINCTUS SAT slumped on his horse as the beast ambled wearily along the road. He felt harried, but that was no new thing, he had felt harried for—for how long had it been? Quite some time. Well before his king had finally and completely banned the practice of "haruspection" as being irretrievably tainted by Paganism, silly old ass, his king. The shadow of the ban had cast itself across the kingdom before it was actually promulgated. What should George Spizzerinctus have done, other than what he actually had done, which was to flee? If that was not too strong a verb, with its implication of action, when, actually, all the haruspex had to do was to go for his usual slow ride, and not come back. And what was he to do now? He was persecuted as though he were a Pagan. Would he seek refuge in what he had heard was still a defiantly Pagan enclave 'x' number of stadia along the road? It had seemed at the time not only the sensible thing to do, but the only thing to do. Now, he was increasingly none too sure. Pagans did not, to be sure, persecute haruspexes as such. But had they not, and might they not, persecute Christians, as such? And thinking of himself, after casually declining some such hospitable offer as it might be, "have some meat offered to idle strangers," being next dipped in a substance and used as a street light, he shivered. Shouts as of a distant crowd crying, "put a lion on Spizzerinctus," came to his dusty ears. Oh dear. Oh dear.

Casting a nervous look around, and perceiving no one in sight, he made the sign of the cross and prayed (nothing wrong with praying in a still, small voice, was there?).

"Oh God of Abraham, Barnabas, and Zebedee, show guidance and a sign to thy servant, George Spizzerinctus. And lead him to the domain of a tolerant and preferably Christian ruler. Amen."

One who would realize that a haruspex was a follower of a science, confound it. Reading the future in livers is a science, confound it!

"Melts, lungs, lights or livers, your honor?" asked a voice.

George looked wildly around to see whose voice this might be which was answering his prayer, for surely, there had been no one about before. There was its source, an old woman squatting by a charcoal brazier over which she turned skewers of meat chunks which sizzled and smoked and sent off a goodly savor. She seemed a clean old woman.

"Take your pick. Nothing like the offals of a fresh killed ram. Rub 'em with a nice clove of garlic if you like, sir, for taste, and to keep away the wampires," while raising her gnarly fingers like a bird's claw, she continued, "Which'll you have, patron? Melts, lights, lungs, or liver? Clean salt for nothing."

George had no doubts as to which he would have. "Liver," he said, firmly opening his purse strings. "All the liver you've got."

"I said all the liver you've got," he repeated, holding out several coins as the old woman held up a single skewer.

But she selected one single small coin and, handing him the one whittled twig with the grilled meat chunks, said, shaking her head, "There, sir, I've got only this one. Business's brisk. I has sold the other liver ones. Can give you melts or lights or lungs. No? So."

Ah, too bad. Hastily, he dismissed his regret, for what God has sent, let him be truly athankful. He rode on a couple of paces so as not to let her see him as he carefully examined his trove. Ahhh. So. Although the liver had been, of course, cut up, no problem. Here was an obvious fragment of the arterial protuberance, there was a definite piece of the venous orifice, the others showed nothing definite one way or the other. Oh, good, benefits. And oh, dear, danger. Oh dear.

Danger from the North. Confound this close chop work she had done. It was not like having an entire fresh liver in front of him, one a man could heft and scan properly. Which North? Northeast? Or Northwest? Or just plain North? Or, heavens.

"Why, mother," he said dolefully, "this liver comes from two clean different rams."

"Mother" threw up both her hands, palms out. "Ah, you've sharp eyes, Sir. Yes. Master killed the two old rams, for they were always fighting each other, and the young ram be enough for our small flock of yews. But, don't you want some garlic, sir? A sprinkle of salt?"

He let her supply both. He said a short, silent grace. He ate.

But he was not happy. Which would come first? The danger, or the benefits? And, danger from the Northwest? Benefits from the Northwest? Or—but it was impossible to say.

A haruspex's life is not a happy one.

II

CHICK WAS HUNGRY, and said so. He had been saying so for some time now, as his master had been for some time late coming home.

"Chick hungry," he announced yet again, in a chittering voice. "Chick wants a plate of nice fresh sardines. Chick wants a plate of nice fresh lampreys. Chick wants a dozen nice fresh dace and chubb and bream and pike and pickerel and Chick wants some nice fresh salmon and Chick wants some oysters and mussels and some sturgeon roes. Chick hungry."

Steps were heard advancing from outside. More than once, the tiles had been cemented, but, somehow, they never stayed cemented. Click-clack-clunk, went the loose tiles. Chick went into an ecstasy of expectation, standing on rear legs and spinning around on his tail and beating untried wings. Then he rushed forward and unsheathed his claws and

assaulted the door, whose inlay of scratches and gouges testi-
fied to many previous periods of impatience. The door
creaked open. Chick flung himself against the newcomer.
"Daddy!" cried Chick. "Daddy, daddy, daddy! I'm hungry!"

"What!" exclaimed Peregrine, batting Chick fondly alongside the head with his rod of office. "What? Hasn't Kit fed
you yet, my dear child?"

More tiles clattered in the opposite direction, in came a
lumbering serving cart with splayed wheels, pushed by an
elderly kitchen thrall, who smiled indulgently.

"He won't eat now if you're not here to feed him."

He began to ladle things into an incredibly dented and battered tin bowl. It would nevertheless have cost a fortune in
the open market, tin being of a very far fetch indeed.

"What have we tonight, Kit?"

"The fish monger says that this is prime plaice tonight.
Would you like a nice piece of fresh plaice, Chick? Jump,
jump, catch."

And all was merry and bright in the official residence of
the Sub-Imperial Sub-Legate of Nova Iguvium, who was
probably the only Sub-Imperial Sub-Legate in the entire
Roman Empire who was raising a dragon chick in his palace.

III

PALADINE PALAEOLOGUS, COMMONLY called King Palindrome, when he was not being commonly called "Last Pagan
King in Lower Europe," was in a walled enclave in the ram-
shackle village which was the capital of his kingdom, Sapodilla. The walled enclave had no name. That is, it had no
other name. Other than the emergency supply of food and
drink, it had no other amenities than that its walls served to
conceal the fact that the king was inside of them.

He did not much like being inside of them.

With the hope of soon being outside of them, he affixed
an eye to the nearest hole in the wall (there were many holes
in the walls). He barely had time to scan the outer scene

when, a shaved second before he ducked, a slung-shot came whizzing through the same hole. Much and for how long had the good old man attempted to use as a guide word, "Live unknown," as others, including some doubtless wiser, had done. "Live unknown, that's the secret," he was known to mutter. "Don't even let them know you're there, er, here. Don't go making vain and gaudy shows of your wealth. Don't be pestiferously proliferating of your advice. Don't tap. Don't nudge. Don't be always or even ever clearing your throat. Don't—" and so on.

This had been advice and counsel for himself as sole surviving Pagan sovereign in Lower Europe, and, as such, it had been good advice and counsel. His tributes to the Empire (Central, or Middle, Roman Empire, to be precise) had been neither the first delivered nor the last. They had neither been ostentatiously lavish and newly wrought nor obviously shabby and hand me down. His tribute bearers had been well instructed neither to slink nor to strut.

But it was hardly advice he could wisely extend to himself in his own domains, and it was quite impossible to carry out in his own grounds. They knew where he was now, all right. He was in his own fortress, run down as it was, and seldom used as it had been. And, tripping and stumbling as the slung shot went whizzing by, he could not keep from swearing aloud. Live unknown indeed. He was still living, but he was certainly not, even as far as his present immediate whereabouts were concerned, unknown. From outside came a shout.

"He's over here, here, on this side. Rufus almost got him. Good shot, Rufus! Come out, come out, you senile old scut, I'll beat your brains bloody!"

"And much inducement that is for me to surrender," muttered the old king. For well he knew the voice which had just cried doom to him. It was that of the youngest heir male of his body lawfully begotten, to wit, Prince Chuck.

"And much do I wish that I never had begotten him," muttered the prince's sire, sucking on a sour tooth, and wondering where he would scuttle next.

"Ah, nor are his full brothers any joy to me. All my bright boys were bastards, damn the laws of me forefathers, anyway." For the laws of his forefathers had required that each and every illegitimate son of a sovereign should, and, indeed, must, on said son's eighteenth birthday, leave the kingdom. Leave it forever, lest, if he remained, treasonous plots be hatched, aiming at the succession of the throne. "And now look what's happened," moaned the stricken sovereign. The laws of the forefathers further required that the bastard on departing be warned that if he ever returned, "either armed, or at the head of an armed multitude," such a one would suffer death.

"Damn the damned law," said Sapodilla's sovereign. "Ah, Perry me boy, where are you, now as I needs you?" For Peregrine had been the last of the love children to leave. Where was he now?

He was in a far country, Nova Umbria it was called, where, in the capital municipum of Nova Iguvium, he occupied the position of Sub-Imperial Sub-Legate of himself, the "August Caesar." True, Peregrine was not too sure just who was "Himself, the August Caesar" right just then.

Outside the walled enclave: "Where is that bloody siege engine?" demanded the voice of Prince Chuck.

Another voice: "It be a coming, Prince, uh, uh, I mean, uh, I mean, King. King! It be a coming, King Chuck."

IV

A LONE HORSEMAN came at a slow pace along the path halfway down a grassy hill. In the clear air the birds called, "bee eaters" swooped and darted. Man and mount seemed toiled and fatigued alike. The horse, which showed good lines, whinnied softly. The rider raised his head and saw a short, thick pony of the shaggy sort, and, sitting next to him on a piece of stone work, a man of almost the same description. The pony was mumbling a mouthful of luscious looking green grass, which did indeed grow all around. The man had merely a blade of it in his fingers, and the fingers moved.

"Hail," said the rider.

As though, almost in answer, there came a loud and piercing squawk. The rider's head jerked up. It rapidly scanned first the sky, and then the ground. But the sound certainly never came from a "bee eater," and neither could he see any other bird from which it might have come. An omen from an invisible creature was not exceedingly useful. Then the rider's cheeks, where stubble had begun to encroach upon what had till very lately been a rather short and well barbered beard, spread into a smile.

"Oh, I say," he said. "That's clever. That's very clever. Oh, do you mind if I ask you how to do it? It is really so very clever."

The squat, shaggy man shrugged, plucked another blade of grass, split it lengthwise, placed it so that the broad side was pressed between his joined thumbs, and blew into the space between them. The squawk was repeated.

The newcomer laughed. "Neat trick," he said. A breeze ruffled his thick, dark hair, revealing a growth of gray beneath.

"My name is George. I'm just wandering about."

"Balbus is mine. P. Grampus Balbus. Build walls."

"Oh, do you? Very useful. I'm afraid that I don't build anything. Not walls, certainly. Although the trade that I practice has been compared by some to building windows."

At having said that much, he began to feel that he had, perhaps, said too much. He tentatively licked a dry, cracked underlip and looked at shaggy P. Grampus Balbus, who appeared to have noticed nothing. After a second, George said, "the way is rather dusty. I wonder if you have any such a thing as a flask of, well, I suppose water would do. Have to, eh?"

In reply, P. Grampus Balbus gestured backwards, behind the stone on which he sat.

"A spring," he said, "the lair of the modest nymph, though it was not here that she saw her Lord, and blushed, and said 'Arthesusa, I am coming!' "

George dismounted, produced a small cup from his pack, knelt, filled the cup, bowed, murmured a brief, quiet grace, bowed, and drank. This done, he led his horse to drink.

"Grampus," he said, "my thanks."

Grampus shrugged again. "Were these still Pagan times, I'd say, 'Thank Jupiter, for 'tis not me, but the rain which fills the spring.' However, since I am a Christian, I will say instead that you should thank God almighty, who created Jupiterael, as well as ourselves."

"What?" said George.

"Well, the beings whom the Pagans mistakenly refer to as gods are, in reality, angels of God almighty, who help Him with His work. At least this is my view."

George found this statement puzzling, but experience had taught him that it is wise to discuss theology with strangers, (and, often, even with friends) as little as possible.

But, P. Grampus Balbus did not attempt to continue the discussion. Instead, he noticed that the two of them had been standing up, and sat down. Then, with a rather powerful tug on George's tunic, he persuaded George to do the same. George did so rather abruptly, and P.G. Balbus murmured in his dusty ear.

"I seem to espy what has all the marks of a pursuit. And as I have no idea why anyone should be pursuing me, I feel that I ought to take the liberty, hope you don't mind, of asking if you have any idea why anyone should be pursuing you?"

And George, seeming rather agitated, said, "Dash it! Damn it! By the Holy Saint Michael, the Satan-binding Archangel, yes I have. I suppose there is nothing for me to do except fling myself upon my horse and ride madly in all directions. All directions, of course, save the one they are coming by. Which one is that, anyway? I can't fall upon my sword, because I don't have it with me. I say, Balbus, what are you doing"

"Building a wall," said Balbus. "Best stand still," he added.

George was not able to assimilate in all detail exactly what was happening. Balbus was walking back and forth, declaiming, declaiming what? Balbus was stopping and chanting, chanting what? Vaguely George thought he heard, as though from a distance, the words, "*Oppidum, oppidum, oppidum* in *agris*," though, perhaps, he did not. And as he watched, he saw the slices of turf rising up and, as though they were building blocks of mason's stone, fit into place, line upon line, bond upon bond, slab upon slab, blocks upon blocks. Soon, very soon, it was dark. What was he to do now? His horse gave a soft sound, the equine version of a yawn. It had been a long, hard ride, and as the beast was certainly not so old as to have to sleep on his feet, the beast lay down. Within the darkness there was a soft, suffused dim light. The horse slept. George shrugged, lay down resting against the beast's back, softly began to recite the Psalms in the Italic version. Then he, too, slept.

Outside of the small hut which Balbus had created, Balbus smoothed his mustache and beard and hair. All were certainly longer than Roman fashion anywhere adhered to, but none were barbarian long. Perhaps a quarter mile off was what appeared to be a decade of troops. He put on a helmet which had been lying on its side. The sight of this evidently gave the decade pause. The decurian himself was observed to put his lance down somewhat before walking up to Balbus and saying, "Are you a Roman officer? Declare yourself, then."

"Priscus Grampus Balbus, an Imperial Pioneer-surveyor of Roman Roads and Walls."

And with that he produced and held up a lead tablet with, presumably, just that information incised upon it. It became quickly evident that the decurian could not be called an omnivores reader. After a moment when his lips moved slowly, and elements of a frown came and went on his sun black, sweat grimed face, an epiphany of sorts was suddenly apparent.

"SPQR!" he exclaimed.

"SPQR!" exclaimed his nine men, rather like an echo.

This was followed by a sort of sigh. Rome and its Empires, the Empire and its Rome, might now be in a permanent decline, but the letters standing for the awesome, time glorified formula, "*Senate Populesque Romanum*," the Senate and the People of Rome, still contained some potent magic and respect. And, for that matter, so did the time glorified concept of Roman Roads and Walls.

However, history, honor, respect, time and glory and all present duty was present duty, and a decurian's duty was to obey the last order received. "Inspector, sir," he said, semi-coining a title that was easy to say, "I am after one George Spizzerinctus, a man who was accused of sorcery and who, having been so accused, immediately fled, thus, of course, proving his guilt. He is believed to be on a black and white gelding. Seen anything of such a one?"

Balbus went deep into thought, then asked, "what color was the man?"

One of the soldiers said, "ruddy."

The Pioneer-surveyor at once shook his head.

"Seen nothing of such a one."

In this he was not telling the whole truth, but he was not under oath, and neither was he lying. The complexion of George Spizzerinctus was so deeply dusty as to disguise all ruddiness.

"However," the decurian, who had swung his horse away, now swung it back. "I did see some dust a bit of a while back, over, ah yes, over there."

So he had. Perhaps the wind.

The decurian hastily and sketchily saluted, then the decade went racing back, hollering and hooting and gesturing towards "over there."

By and by, even the dust of the troop movements had dissipated. The Pioneer-surveyor took up his sword again and slashed a curve in the hillside so thoroughly ignored by the military.

"Well, well, George Spizzerinctus, accused sorcerer, you may come out now."

"I may? May I? Thank you. I shall. That was well done indeed."

"When Balbus builds a wall," said Balbus, "he builds it well."

"I can see that," said George, "but now that you know that I've been accused of sorcery, you won't think less of me, will you?"

Balbus laughed. "After what you've seen me do? Don't you think that would be a little bit like the ocean telling the river it was wet?"

"True," said George, "and since that is the case, I may as well speak to you honestly. I don't know where to go. When I reach a fork in the road, lacking a liver to read, I don't even know whether to turn right or left. I am not really a sorcerer, just a man who can read the future in the animal's liver. But Christian kings do consider my trade to be sorcery. I greatly fear, however, that I will not be treated more kindly by the Pagans, for my personal faith is that of a Christian."

"When you get to a crossroad," said Balbus, "I suggest you make the sign of the cross," he quickly did so, "and say a prayer to Hecatael for guidance. As for the rest, your situation is very similar to my own." He stopped to rub some dust out of his eyes, wiped his nose on his sleeve, and continued.

"I, however, have a solution which you might also wish to adopt. There is a place not very far away called Nova Umbria, where there is complete freethought of religion." He looked towards the horizon. "The Christians, Jews, and Pagans in this place live in harmony. They have realized that they all venerate the divine essence which permeates everything, and that the details of how they do so are of relatively little importance. I have a map which tells how to reach this place, and you, if you like, are welcome to join me."

"Certainly," said Spizzerinctus, "I've always said that when you don't have a whole liver handy, a good map is the next best thing."

V

KIT'S FORMAL POSITION was only that of kitchen thrall, but
Peregrine was not a snob. The old man had lived in Nova
Iguvium for a long time, and knew nearly everyone. So, in
exchange for giving Kit a little time off now and then to visit
with his family and friends, Kit gave Peregrine regular re-
ports on the important happenings of the city. Peregrine,
however, was not always happy with what he heard. "First of
all," said Kit, "the people are grumbling because they miss
the cock fights."

"Let them grumble," said Peregrine. "So long as I am
Sub-Legate, there will be no pointless torturing of birds in
Nova Umbria. I don't mind them killing birds for food. Birds
eat other birds, after all. *But* to strap sharp bits of metal to
their feet and then push them into a fight, no, I won't tolerate
it."

"With respect, sir, they seem to think you're just a little
bit odd when it comes to things that fly. They know that
you've commissioned every good artist in Nova Umbria to
sculpt, or paint, or carve images of birds in flight."

"So I have," said Peregrine. He looked around his throne
room, where dozens of such images sat amongst the piles of
dust from the mildewed, crumbling stones. "Perhaps I am
having some difficulty changing from being a wanderer to
being Sub-Legate, and looking at these birds gives me a feeling of freedom."

This was true. Peregrine was having trouble adjusting to
staying in one place so long. The desire to move still pulled
at him. And although he didn't remember much from the
time he had spent as a falcon, (since falcons don't remember
things in the same way that people do) there was one
memory which was embedded in his mind. That was the
feeling he'd had when he had flown through the air. No other
experience had ever provided him with that kind of exhilara-
tion.

"Then there's your name, which, of course, means falcon."

"They knew my name when they made me Sub-Legate."

"You know how fickle the crowds can be. Next is the fact that you first came to us on the wings of a dragon."

"They knew that, too."

"Sir, if my report upsets you, I'll stop."

"No, please go on."

"Well, finally, there is the fact that you keep a dragon chick in your palace."

"They are lucky to have a ruler who is guilty of no greater crimes than these."

"I quite agree. But you know how people talk. There have even been some who have used the word 'sorcerer'."

"I wish I was one. Hey, is there any of that plump pork left?"

"Yes, Sub-Legate."

Peregrine heard a knock at the door. Since Kit was busy cooking, and there were no other servants around, he descended the narrow staircase himself, taking care not to trip on the loose stones, and opened the large oak and iron door. It was the fish monger, with his wagon full.

"I have some very good pike today," said the fish monger. He held a large one in his right hand for inspection. With his left hand, he rubbed his bent, fish oil soaked fingers against his dry, flaking skin. "It's quite fresh."

Peregrine looked at the fish, took a breath, and determined that it was, if perhaps not quite fresh, at least not quite rotten.

"Thank you. I'm sure Chick will love it."

"I'm sure he will. Urn, I'd like to speak to you honestly, sir, if you don't object."

"Go ahead."

"Well, your dragon child is growing, and, like any growing boy, he has a good appetite that gets better whenever he grows, which, it seems to me, he does just about every day."

"That's sure true. It's a good thing I don't have to buy him clothes as well as fish."

"Indeed. But the amount of fish he eats keeps growing, too. Of course, we're all grateful that this dragon eats only fish, rather than four legged animals, or even human beings."

"What's your point?"

"Well, providing you with so much fish is becoming somewhat difficult."

"Don't I pay you enough?"

"Certainly. But, here in Nova Iguvium, there's more to business than just money. There's a lot of people in this city that I've been selling fish to since I was a boy. They aren't just my customers, they're my friends. Their parents used to buy fish from my papa when he was a boy. It's not so easy to just say 'sorry, I can't sell you my fish anymore. The Sub-Legate pays better.' "

"I understand. I'm glad you told me. I'll teach Chick to fish for himself as soon as I can."

"Thank you, Sub-Legate," said the fish monger. But to himself he thought, from where will this dragon take his fish, if not from the same river where our fishermen take theirs?

Peregrine went upstairs to collect some coins to pay for the fish.

"I know I left a purse with gold coins here." he muttered. I'd hate, he thought, to think that Kit is stealing from me.

Then, another thought flashed into his mind. He walked down the hall and into the large room where Chick lived. Even though the window was kept open, and the chamber maid cleaned the room every day, it still smelled strongly of fish. He grabbed the large stone which Chick kept next to his bed and rolled it aside. Behind it was the leather purse, containing several gold coins.

"Bad Chick," said Peregrine. "Haven't I told you not to steal?"

He tapped him lightly with his rod of office.

"Chick sorry," said the no longer little dragon. "They were so shiny pretty. Chick wanted to look."

Instinctive treasure hoarding behavior, thought Peregrine. Can one train a cat not to hunt smaller animals? Can one teach a dog not to urinate on trees? Can one bring up a boy in such a way that he will not seek sexual gratification?

One can try, but one is likely to be disappointed.

He reached into his pocket and pulled out a few copper coins.

They weren't worth much, but they were shiny.

"You can have these."

"Thank you. Thank you." Chick did a quick whirl on his tail to express his pleasure, then grabbed the coins and placed them behind the rock. While he was rolling it back into place, Peregrine went back down the stairs, had the fish loaded into a barrel, and paid the fish monger.

"Kit, will you help me carry these fish upstairs?"

"Certainly, your Excellency."

They carried the barrel up the stairs, down the hall, and into Chick's room. Chick saw the barrel. His red eyes widened, and he opened his jaws, revealing slippery white fangs. He exhaled rapidly, releasing a gust of warm, fishy breath. He started jumping up and down. The floor shook, a cloud of dust filled the air, and chunks of stone could be heard falling from the walls. They tipped the fish into the tin bowl, and Chick began grabbing them and stuffing them into his mouth. His eyes were almost completely closed in rapture as he noisily chewed and swallowed the fish. An occasional head or tail fell to the floor.

"If you'll excuse me," said Kit, "I have to finish preparing your dinner."

Peregrine watched the little dragon eat. He still thought of Chick that way, as "the little dragon." When he had hatched, he had been about the size of a cat. But now he was bigger than Peregrine himself.

When the dragon had stopped eating, Peregrine decided to speak.

"Chick," he said, "there are a couple of things I have to tell you."

"What, daddy?"

"Well, first of all, you're getting bigger. Soon, you won't be able to fit through the doors. Then you'll have to live somewhere else."

"But where, daddy?" The young dragon looked frightened.

"Well, I suppose I can have a tent set up next to the castle."

"All right, daddy."

"There's another thing. You'll have to start learning to fish for yourself."

"Where, daddy?"

"In the river. It's not far away."

"Will you teach me?"

"Certainly."

"All right, daddy."

Chick finished his dinner less gleefully. Peregrine went to his dining room to have his. Chick followed.

As Peregrine ate the roasted pig, Chick looked into the mirror. It seemed that Peregrine's words had put him into a contemplative mood.

"Daddy likes to eat meat."

"Yes," said Peregrine. He stuffed some into his mouth.

"I don't like meat."

"That's why I give you fish."

"Do you eat fish?"

"I like it now and then, but not for every meal."

"Why?" He looked puzzled.

"I don't know. I've never been all that fond of fish."

Chick pointed a claw at his scaly arm and said, "Green."

"That's right."

He pointed at Peregrine. "Not green."

"No. I suppose I'm sort of a pinkish tan."

"Different."

"Yes."

"Why different?"

Peregrine had known that this question would come up eventually.

"Well you see, you're a dragon, and I'm a human being."

Chick's forehead wrinkled. He looked puzzled.

"Why?"

"That's just the way it is. Most dragons are raised by other dragons. But you were raised by people because your dragon parents aren't around."

"There are other dragons?"

"Certainly."

"Can Chick play with them?" He made a gleeful half-twirl.

"No, I'm afraid not."

Chick frowned.

"Why?"

"Most dragons don't like people much."

"Why?"

"They just don't. Besides, most dragons live in caves way up in the mountains."

"How do they get up in the mountains?"

"They fly."

"How?"

"With their wings."

Peregrine gently tapped Chick's left wing with his staff of office.

"Like a bird?"

"Exactly."

Chick looked at his wings, then looked around the room at the many images of birds in flight. His large reddish eyes seemed to widen with sudden comprehension. He stretched his wings, flapped them, and rose into the air. He rose until his head hit the ceiling, then he fell to the floor.

"I don't like flying. Flying hurts." He licked his wings and folded them tightly.

"You can't fly in here. You have to go outside."

"Can we go now?"

"Well, all right."

He got up from the table, leaving the rest of the roast pork for Kit to eat. They walked down the stairs, Chick rather more rapidly than Peregrine. In his enthusiasm, Chick tripped on the broken stair, then got back up without even a whimper. When he reached the bottom, he started to jump up and down with excitement. But, he didn't flap his wings.

He waited until Peregrine was outside, and then he stretched and flapped his large, leathery wings. He flapped them more and more rapidly until, gradually, he started to leave the ground. He circled, he rose, he descended, he went into a glide, a long, slow, very slow glide, and then he climbed higher into the sky, and higher and higher, until he was just a tiny spot, and then that spot disappeared. For a moment, Peregrine thought that he would not come back. But then the spot reappeared, and began to grow larger and larger again. And then, Chick landed.

"Flying is fun." The young dragon grinned gleefully.

"I'm glad you like it."

"Come fly with me."

"People can't fly."

"You can."

"No, I can't."

"Yes you can."

Chick flapped his wings, rose into the air again, swooped down and picked Peregrine up with his long, thin, front paws. Suddenly, it was the objects on the ground which were getting smaller and smaller. He saw his castle shrink, and he looked down on the houses and temples and churches and narrow roads of the city. Then these receded into the distance, and were replaced by huts and fields and livestock and small, simple shrines. Then these gave way to open, grassy plains, greenish brown hills, a river, and the dark, thick forest of oak.

At first, Peregrine was frightened. Chick is still a child, he thought, he might accidentally drop me. But then he relaxed, and he realized that he had finally achieved what he had been wanting so badly. Once again, he was flying.

Still, best not to overdo it the first time.

"I think you'd better take me home now," he finally said.

"All right, daddy."

Chick reversed his course. Peregrine savored the feeling of the wind on his skin, knowing that it would soon end. Presently, he saw the familiar streets below him again, and his own palace among them.

Below, the people looked up at the sky.

"What sort of bird is that?"

"Idiot, that's not a bird. That's our Sub-Legate, being carried through the air in the arms of his dragon."

"Oh."

"He came to us on the wings of a dragon, and now he is riding one again. Damned odd, I'd say."

"Damned odd. Normal people don't go around riding dragons."

"They don't."

This is what the Pagans were saying. The Christians, however, were not so kind.

"It's just as I said before," said Father Paolus. "He is the AntiChrist, as predicted by the prophet John in the book of Revelations, who will come to us accompanied by a great dragon. Both the man and the dragon are manifestations of the great beast, which is, of course, Satan himself."

"What should we do?" asked Brother Pier.

"Clearly, we must fight him in any way we can, whether by word or by deed. We are soldiers of Christ."

"But how? Many of the people in these parts are either Pagan or Jews. Pagans and Jews are a godless bunch. They don't believe in AntiChrist."

"No. But they do have a natural fear of sorcerers. And of dragons."

And so, the two emissaries of Christ went to the public square, where many farmers who had come to town to sell their crops were relaxing before making the trip home. They spoke the word, and did not find their fellow citizens to be entirely unreceptive.

"We strain under the burden of our Sub-Legate's taxes," began Father Paolus, "and why? To pay the fish monger to deliver the fish which once fed our families, into the jaws of that dragon beast."

"It's unnatural," said one of his listeners, a man who had come into town to sell parsnips, and had already spent much of his earnings on mead. "Dragons and people aren't meant to live together." He opened his mouth and squirted another jet of the sweet burning liquid into his mouth from a hairy gray goat-skin flask.

"You're right," shouted Brother Pier, "it violates the laws of nature!"

"He says he's gonna teach the dragon to fish for himself," said the fish monger.

"And where will those fish be taken from?" asked Father Paolus. "Will it not be from the same rivers which our families get their nourishment from? The only thing that will change is that then the families of the fishermen will go hungry as well."

"You know what I heard?" said an elderly man who leaned on a thick oak cane with a small wrinkled face carved into it, "I heard that dragons everywhere are starting to cause trouble. All over Rome."

"Indeed they are," said Father Paolus. "Dragons who were once content to eat trash fish now consume the good fish. Dragons who once were satisfied to engage in ritualized attempts to steal treasure are now really stealing it. And as they leave with a belly full of fish and an armful of gold, they have been heard to say, 'Uprising. Revolt. Revolution.' " And now, seeing that the growing crowd was receptive, he grew still bolder and said, "And perhaps the time has come for us to start saying the same thing."

George Spizzerinctus and P. Grampus Balbus passed the noisy crowd, but, sensing an angry mood, they avoided it and walked instead to the crumbling palace of the Imperial Sub-Legate.

Spizzerinctus hesitated, so Balbus knocked on the door.

Peregrine sat on the throne, exhilarated by his flight with Chick. The dragon rested beside him. Peregrine heard the knock.

"Kit, would you answer the door?"

"Certainly, Sub-Legate."

Kit went down the stairs, then came back up.

"Two men want to see you. I wouldn't let them in though, sir. They're both strangers. They have rather long hair and beards, and they're both, well, filthy."

"Show them in."

"As you wish."

He disappeared again, and reappeared with two men who did, indeed, fit the description. Their hair and beards were not only long, but tangled, and were the same color as their skin and clothing, the reddish brown of the road. But Peregrine recalled that he and his traveling companions had once looked the same way.

"My name," said the first, "is Priscus Grampus Balbus." He lifted his arm to point to his companion. The smell of stale sweat filled the room. "My friend's name is George Spizzerinctus. We have traveled a long way because we have heard that this is a place where Pagans, Christians and Jews live together in perfect harmony, because they have realized that they all venerate the divine essence which permeates everything, and that the details of how they do so are relatively unimportant."

"Horse apples," said Peregrine. "The Pagans, Christians and Jews here despise each other. But a representative of Caesar Augustus told them that they have to tolerate each other. And so did I. So, they tolerate each other. Barely."

"Oh," said Spizzerinctus. "Well, still, at least the Sub-Legate is an enlightened man, willing, perhaps, to tolerate," he paused, but decided that he had to take a chance, "a Christian who makes his living by reading the future in animal's livers."

"I've heard of haruspexism," said Peregrine, "but I never quite understood how it works."

"Well, your Excellency, if you provide me with a whole liver, I can demonstrate."

"Kit, do we still have the liver from that pig we slaughtered?"

"Yes, Sub-Legate."

Kit produced the liver, which was sitting in congealing blood on a battered, rusty iron plate, then left the room. George contemplated the veins and arteries and deposits of fat.

"The direction of the veins," said Spizzerinctus, as he ran a blood stained finger across the dark blue line, "indicate the direction of your good fortune. According to this vein, if his

Excellency wants good fortune, he should travel first west, then north, then northwest, then, hm, west again."

Peregrine thought about that for a moment, then said, "that would lead me right back to the kingdom of my birth."

"Then that," said Spizzerinctus, as he absentmindedly licked the blood off his fingertips, "is where your good fortune lies, although," he paused, "oh dear, this ridge of fat tells me that you won't achieve it without overcoming an obstacle at the end of your journey."

"That doesn't surprise me," said Peregrine. "In the kingdom where I was born, I am the bastard son of a king. And in that kingdom, there is a law which states that every bastard son of a king must leave at the age of eighteen, and never return, or face death."

"I only know what the organ tells me," said George.

Outside, the two men of the cloth continued their sermon.

"If we don't act now," said Father Paolus, "the dragon will be too large. We won't possibly be able to overcome it."

"For that matter," said a plump farmer's wife, "how can we overcome it now?"

"We will need somebody who can go into the castle. Somebody whom the Sub-Legate knows. Somebody who has a reason to go in."

"But who?"

"How about the fish monger?"

"Me?" said the fish monger. "He's never been mean to me."

"How do you plan to earn a living after the dragon has learned to fish for himself, and there are no more fish for you to sell?"

"You know," he said after a moment, "I've been thinking about that myself."

"Then you can help us defeat the dragon. You visit the castle every day. Does the dragon have any weaknesses?"

"Yes. He does have one."

VI

"KIT," SAID PEREGRINE, "Would you open the door?"

"Yes, Sub-Legate."

He walked out, then back up. With him was the fish monger.

"First," said the fish monger, "I want to say that I'm sorry about what I said earlier. I have no right to complain about a customer who pays me with coins like these."

He pulled a leather purse out of his pocket, opened it, and the light caught the shiny gold. Chick looked up. The dragon's red eyes glinted.

He put the purse back in his pocket.

"Second, I wanted to say that I can't work tomorrow, so I brought some extra fish today. There's rather a lot of it sir, so could you all come out and help me carry it?"

"These men aren't my servants," said Peregrine.

"I'd be happy to help you carry the fish, Sub-Legate," said Spizzerinctus.

"So would I," said Balbus, "for fish are the symbol of my Lord, Jesus Christ, who commanded the angel Neptunael to support His weight as He walked across the water."

"Thank you, kind travelers," said the fish monger.

They walked down the stairs, followed by the fish monger, who reached into his pocket and gently pulled the leather purse up until it fell to the ground with a soft clank.

To the extent that a dragon is able to creep, Chick crept up and snatched the purse. He then ran down the hallway towards his room.

"Watch out for that loose stone," said Peregrine. "I almost broke my leg on it." Then, suddenly, he exclaimed, "Neptunael?"

"Certainly," said Balbus. "The angel whom God gave dominion over all the oceans. It was he, also, whom Moses called upon to part the Red Sea."

"It's right there," said the fish monger.

"Where?"

"See that cart loaded with barrels?"

Peregrine, Spizzerinctus, Balbus and Kit walked out the door and towards the barrels. The fish monger, however, did not walk out the door and towards the barrels. Instead, he walked back into the door and locked it from the inside.

"Hey, wait," said Peregrine, "I don't under—"

But as he saw the mob approaching, he very quickly did understand.

Barrel staves, bung starters, wagon tongues, forge hammers, wash poles, and other rude objects had been more or less instantly converted into weaponry. Those who had none managed without too much difficulty by prying up the stone seats of the stoa and the blocks from nearby shops and streets. Sundry chunks of marble from unfinished gravestones and graven images filled the hands of the boiling mob in ready position to hurl their anger.

The fish monger ran back up the stairs, raced down the hall to where Chick was trying to quietly roll a large stone away from the wall, and bolted the thick, metal studded wooden door shut from the outside.

Crumbling though the castle was, its doors, and the locks on those doors were repaired quite regularly.

"I think," said George, "that this might be a good time to build another wall."

"I think," said Balbus, "that I'm inclined to agree."

Again, P. Grampus Balbus picked up a stick and drew lines on the ground. Again, there were the chants, the incantations and the prayers half mumbled.

Nothing happened.

The angry mob moved closer.

"It seems," said Balbus, "that I need some extra help."

Balbus drew a circle around himself in the dirt, drew a cross within the circle, crossed himself, mumbled a few prayers to each of the four directions, and then began to sing in a loud, deep, clear voice:

> "Blessed angel Gaiael,
> Mistress of the earthly realm.
> I have need for you today.
> Build me bricks out of your clay."

And again, the earth began to rise up, and to form itself into bricks and mortar, piling up one on top of another until the castle was surrounded by a great, high wall. Earth worms wriggled on the surface of some of the bricks, and several confused gophers crawled out of others and fell to the ground. This time, however, Balbus did not build a roof.

"That," said Balbus, "was the doing of the oldest angel of them all."

"What did I tell you?" said Father Paolus. "It's sorcery."

"I have to get back into the castle," said Peregrine, "I could climb through that open window if I could reach it."

"I don't know how to build stairs," said Balbus, "but I think I can do something almost as good. Stand next to the castle, under the open window."

Peregrine did, and the chants, incantations, and prayers were mumbled once again. Peregrine felt the ground under him start to rise. And it kept rising until he was right next to the open window. It was then easy to crawl through. He heard a wailing coming from Chick's room.

"Daddy, daddy. Chick can't open the door. Let Chick out. Chick sorry I stole again. Please, let Chick out!"

Peregrine ran down the hallway and opened the door. Chick came out, tears streaming from his even more reddish than usual eyes, down the scales of his face and into his open mouth. He held the purse of coins between the claws of the long, bony fingers of his extended hand.

"Chick sorry, daddy. I won't steal again."

Peregrine grabbed the purse and stuffed it into his pocket.

"We'll talk about that later," he said. "Right now, I'm going to need your help."

They rushed down the stairs, and out the door. From behind the new wall, cries could be heard of: "Kill the sorcerer" and "get the dragon lover!"

The crowd soon realized that the wall was not made of stone, but merely of clay. They set to work hitting it with axes, picks, shovels, and knives. Clods of dirt flew through the air. But the farmers were used to breathing dust. They worked cheerfully, sweating a little, and passing around some of the mead, wine, and ale that they had just purchased. Some of them started singing work songs.

"How many people," Peregrine asked the young dragon, "can you lift and still fly?"

"Chick doesn't know," said Chick. He looked worried.

"I'll stay behind," said Kit, "most of them are my friends. They won't hurt me."

"Thank you," said Peregrine. Then, to Chick, "Do you think you can fly with three people?"

"Chick doesn't know."

"Can you try?"

"Chick might drop them."

"Just try it."

"All right, daddy."

Chick grabbed Peregrine with one long, thin arm. He clasped George and Grampus with the other. He began to flap his wings. He breathed deeply, gritted his long fangs, and began to slowly rise into the air. Gradually he climbed higher, then went into a glide over the wall, over the screaming mob, and away, towards the thick, green forest of oak.

The crowd let out a collective moan when they saw that their quarry was escaping.

"The power of the Satan," said Father Paolus, "is greater than I had imagined."

But the crowd was disappointed that the adventure had not gone as they had planned. And, besides being disappointed, they were angry.

"There he goes again, talking about the Satan," said a voice.

"Didn't he used to say that our gods, the gods of our ancestors, were agents of his Satan?"

"Yeah. And we weren't allowed to have our festivals."

"And they threw their garbage into our temples."

"My friends," said Father Paolus, "let us not forget why we are here. To join forces against a common enemy."

But now the common enemy was gone, and the crowd no longer seemed to be listening.

VII

"IT'S A GOOD thing I have those gold coins," said Peregrine. "They'll feed us for a while. Of course, Chick will have to start fishing for himself."

"The *piscine* isn't far away," said Balbus, "but there are no merchants selling roast pork in these woods. Perhaps I'll say a prayer to Dianael, and then we can try to catch some rabbits."

"Just when I thought I'd found a home," said Spizzerinctus, "I'm a fugitive again."

"As are we all," said Balbus. He swatted a biting fly that had landed on his nose. "Damn these bugs. Smoke would help keep them away."

"I'm cold anyway," said Spizzerinctus. "There's plenty of dry wood. Let's build a fire."

They gathered some dead branches into a pile. Balbus put his hands into his pockets.

"Damn it. My flint lock must have fallen out while we were flying."

"That's all right," said Peregrine. "Chick can start the fire."

"But, daddy," said Chick, "you told Chick not to breath fire."

"This time it's OK," said Peregrine.

"All right daddy."

The dragon shrugged, tensed his shoulders, took in a deep breath, and exhaled quickly. Reddish orange flames shot from his mouth and nose to the pile of wood, igniting it into a blazing smoky fire that smelled very much like a fish dinner in rather early stages of preparation. The four travelers gathered around it and warmed their hands.

"You know," said George, "I still remember what I saw in that liver. You're supposed to return to the place of your birth. And I think that the liver was speaking to everyone who was in the room. We're supposed to follow you home."

"Well," said Peregrine, "you might follow me onto the end of a spear if we go there on foot. But we could fly over the old kingdom, just to look at it. Chick, do you think you could fly with us again?"

"Yes," said Chick proudly, "that wasn't hard for Chick."

VIII

KING PALADINE PALAEOGUS had seen to it that his walled enclave was stocked full of things to eat, dried and pickled meat, vegetables and fruit, grains and beans and barrels of water and wine. He had done so in order to be prepared for the possibility of an enemy attack. He had recently been very glad that he had done so. It had never, however, occurred to him that the enemy from whom he would be hiding would be his own lawful sons.

But hide from them he had. The security of the high, thick, slippery wall was great enough that he had been able to get an occasional bit of troubled sleep. But now the food, and the wine, and even the water were all gone. Paladine knew that even if his sons did not manage to break through the walls, there would soon be no choices left but to surrender or fall on his sword—which, unfortunately, was not as sharp as it could have been.

The old man delicately turned his head and looked into the sky. He realized that hunger and thirst must already be making him delirious. He saw, he thought he saw, a strange shadow. And then he heard, he was sure he heard, the beating of mighty wings. And then he saw, he was certain he saw, a small dragon wobbling through the sky with three large men in its arms. And one of them looked just like Perry.

From the air, Peregrine looked down in amazement at the scene below. Prince Chuck and his brothers, along with a small group of armed rabble-rousers, were assaulting the enclave. Once again, he witnessed a wall being attacked, this time with battering rams, catapults, and anything else available. And they did seem to be gradually wearing the old wall down. It might not be much longer, it seemed to Peregrine, before they managed to break through.

"My wings are tired," whimpered Chick.

"That's all right," said Peregrine, "We're here. Just land inside those walls. That man down there is my daddy."

"Daddy has a daddy?"

Chick spiraled downwards, silently gliding in ever diminishing concentric circles towards Paladine's direction, then landed. Peregrine jumped to the ground, followed by his companions.

"Hello papa."

"Perry! It is you!"

"Yes. I hope you're not angry with me for breaking the laws of our ancestors."

"If I ever sit on the throne again, my first act as king will be to take the texts containing the laws of our ancestors, dip them in human excrement and other such foul ingredients, and promptly burn them. Which is my way of saying 'welcome back!' I wish I had all my bastards back. As for my lawful sons . . ." his voice trailed off. But Peregrine saw that his face had turned ruddy just thinking about them.

They embraced, and Peregrine said, "Don't worry. You will sit on the throne again, Papa."

"How? Even with a small dragon on our side, there's too many of them to fight hand to hand. They have sharp swords and spears and iron-headed arrows that could go through even his skin."

"True. But it will take them a moment to realize that. The first thing they'll do when confronted with a dragon is panic."

"And then?" asked Paladine.

"They will be where we now stand."

Peregrine whispered something into Chick's ear. The dragon grinned, showing his large, white fangs, nodded his head, and snickered steamily. Then Peregrine undid the lock on the enclave's door and flung it open.

"What're you doing?" screamed Paladine.

"Oh dear," muttered Spizzerinctus.

Balbus froze for a moment, then crossed himself, then mumbled, "Blessed angel Persephoneal, please carry my soul to God and not to Hades."

Chick let out a chuckle and a hiss, then grabbed the four men, deftly folded two under each arm, flapped his wings, rose into the air, climbed higher, and carried them over the wall. Then he descended, circled low, and landed with them behind the group of rebels. Peregrine drew his sword and let out a yell. Chick spread his wings, roared, showed his teeth, and issued forth a whoosh of breath and flame, ending with a slightly fishy belch. He ran towards the men. The men screamed and ran in all directions.

"Men," shouted Prince Chuck, "we must keep control of our wits. Look, the walled enclave is unlocked. We can bar ourselves inside, and they won't be able to get us."

The rebels looked at the wall and saw that the door was indeed open. In their haste, they did not remember that the young dragon had wings, and that the enclave had no roof. They ran in and bolted the iron gate shut.

"And now," said Peregrine, "let's find a nice, large rock to roll against the door."

They did so before Prince Chuck and his men realized that they had been tricked.

IX

"IT'S GREAT TO see you again," said Peregrine.

"It's great to be seen," said Paladine, who was busily eating and drinking in order to make up for his days of deprivation. "It's great to have fresh meat again, too. Mmmmm. Roast pork. Good enough for Homer, good enough for me; pickled pork indeed." He grimaced at the memory of his recent hardships.

"Hid in the hypocaust at first, but they smoked me out. Speaking of the hypocaust, this room is damned chilly." He turned towards a servant and bellowed, "can't you feel the cold? Start a fire in the hypocaust, you fool." The servant scuttled away towards the cellar.

Chick was sliding cod and herring down his long, black, bifurcated tongue.

Spizzerinctus grabbed the roast pig's liver and studied the arteries, while stuffing meat into his mouth.

Peregrine poured a little wine onto the floor and toasted, "for the gods," then emptied the rest of the glass into his mouth.

Balbus poured a little wine on the floor, emptied the rest of the glass into his mouth, then mumbled, "the blood of Bachael."

"You seem like a very decent sort of king," said Spizzerinctus, "what's your name?"

"His name's Paladine," said Peregrine, "although some people call him King Palindrome."

"Why?"

"Because he's very fond of palindromes."

"Really?" said George. "Did you know that the first words that human beings ever spoke were palindromes?"

"They were?" said Paladine.

"Yes, indeed. Adam walked up to Eve and said, 'Madam, I'm Adam.' Her reply was, 'Eve.' "

"Oh, that is quite good," exclaimed the king, his face breaking into a grin, "but why do you say that these were the first words ever spoken by human beings?"

"He doesn't know that story," said Peregrine. "He's a Pagan. But don't worry. You won't be used to light up the streets at night, or nourish large cats."

"What? Fancy such a notion!" said Paladine. "You certainly won't. Not as long as I'm the 'Last Pagan King of Lower Europe!' "

"Or I!" said Peregrine.

"Perhaps," interjected Balbus, "we could join together in an ecumenical sort of prayer?"

"Perhaps," said Spizzerinctus, "*if* it has nothing blasphemous about it."

"And nothing that betrays the gods of our ancestors," added Paladine.

"How about this?" said Balbus, "we call upon the life force which permeates all things to grant to this kingdom, to the men, women and children, to the beasts and fruits thereof, success in word and deed, before and behind, and in public, in vow and sacrifice. Be favorable and propitious with thy peace, and keep us safe. Keep safe the magistrates, the priesthoods, the plebs, and the lives of all creatures of fields and fruits and bees and hives. O, though and those who be invoked, we invoke thee, in truth, we invoke thee."

"Amen," said Spizzerinctus.

"So mote it be," added Peregrine.

"I say," said Paladine, "I believe that was rather touching. Felt touched, I say."

"Felt so myself," smiled Spizzerinctus.

Chick carefully balanced a herring on his snout, and let it slide slyly down his smiling, toothy mouth.

~ ~ ~ ~ ~

INTRODUCTION

INTRODUCTION

Ethan Davidson

Avram and I wrote this story together in the early eighties. At the time, I lived on Polk Street, and he occasionally visited me there. When I reread it I realized that it had become, among other things, a nostalgia piece about the Polk Street, and the San Francisco, that once was. While some of the things described in the story still happen in the small hours of the night, most of the low-income eccentrics have been forced out. Polk Street, like most of the rest of San Francisco, has been massively gentrified. There is, however, a Seventies themed bar, with a waterbed inside it. I recall no waterbeds in the Polk Street bars I visited in the actual 1970s.

THE SAFETY OF A LARGER HERD

Avram Davidson & Ethan Davidson

DWAYNE WALKED UP the street slowly. He liked to check out the action on Polk Street at night. He didn't participate much, but he liked to watch. Castro Street, despite being the center of San Francisco's large gay community, bored him. It was too clean, too bourgeoisie, too middle class. To him, the lower key, seamier, only partially gay scene on Polk Street struck him as more interesting. On the other hand, it wasn't as intense as the Tenderloin, where every square foot of space was inhabited by the crazy, the dangerous, the dangerously crazy, the drunk and stoned who hustled and begged for your money, your body, your cigarettes, your time, and whatever else of yours they could. Your pocket comb. Your soul. That scene was a little too heavy. To him, Polk Street seemed just about right.

Right now he was just emerging from the Tenderloin region. Alongside him strolled a rather cute Latina transsexual hooker wearing a low-cut blouse, a miniskirt, and fishnet stockings. This one approached a couple of other girls of similar description. Upon seeing her, one of the girls chimed in a cheerful singsong voice, "the police are looking for you."

"Fuck you," came the civil-toned reply.

"The police are looking for you," she repeated, apparently in a jolly mood, "because remember that time you killed that old lady? And burned her purse and wallet? With the needles inside it?"

Jesus, Dwayne thought, it's probably all a joke, but looking at them, it seemed like it could all be true. Whoever thought effeminacy was always accompanied by squeamishness towards all things violent (i.e., "manly") had never been acquainted with street queens like these. He quickly walked by just as one turned to him with a "hey handsome."

Around a shop which specialized in magazines with large, clear photographs of men with names like "Lance" and "Rod", books with titles like "Horse Play" and "Puppy Love", and movies, for twenty five cents per minute, with titles like "Porn in the U.S.A." and "A Hard Gay's Night", he passed the usual crowd of less exotic male prostitutes. These were the teen-age boys known as "chickens." While some were effeminate, most looked quite similar to the boys of the same age who lived in suburbs all over America, with longish hair, jeans, radios, and T-shirts advertising their favorite heavy metal bands. Most were runaways and drifters who just did it for the money, and many did not think of themselves as gay. But they usually squandered most of the money on drugs, which insured that they would have to do it again, soon. They definitely had a sleazy air about them, or they soon developed one. And, of course, wherever you found the younger men called chickens, you were sure to find the older men called chicken hawks. You didn't find either in the respectable streets or suburbs. At least not openly in character.

Next to one of the large, old-fashioned family-owned markets, which had survived the coming of the chain supermarkets as well as all the subsequent changes, Dwayne saw one of the local "crazies," talking loudly to himself in the street.

"My name is Crown Prince Euphoria. All diseases are in reality caused by yeast infections. To cure yourself, bathe in your own urine or drink it. A golden shower in the fountain of youth. Praise Jesus. Hallelujah."

Dwayne had spent some time watching this fellow and had concluded that, for whatever reason, he was pretending to be a lot crazier than he really was, and that he knew more about what was going on than he led one to believe. Maybe he was just thinking out loud, not always a safe pastime out on Maple Street in Suburban Grove—and maybe he just had a "crazy shtick."

He reflected that as Castro Street had taken over the role of gay mecca, Polk Street had become something of a mecca for those who were not dramatically weird, but were nevertheless somehow odd. It seemed to be the best place for such marginal types to fit in without being noticed. "I am here because I seek the safety of a larger herd," an old meth-freak used to say. And say. And—

To be sure, no one stared at "Poor little Mary Swift" back in Black Hawk Hill, Iowa (pop. 1500), but Mary found Black Hawk Hill very dull. And in Des Moines, they did stare. So she wound up in San Francisco. On Polk Street. Every two weeks, the letter and the check. "Oh I do hope you are all right Mary dear, mother worries so." And so mother did. And perhaps, all the same, perhaps mother was just a little bit relieved, too.

Now Dwayne entered one of the more interesting places to meet different odd types; an unnamed bar whose low prices reflected the fact that it was pretty much Polk Street's only "straight" saloon. The clientele? Mostly the middle-aged or even old, with men and women equally visible. But the air of a neighborhood bar in any old town was misleading. Those who were there were there for a good reason. You wouldn't expect, generally speaking, a man well into his sixties to tell you about his frequent youthful sniffing of amyl nitrate.

Would you?

Would you say that Dwayne was a little nosy?

Dwayne was a little nosy.

He started on a vodka and tonic and hoped to strike up a conversation with the fellows next to him, who were just slightly odd, if you happened to consider the matter, and in some way that he had never before quite seen. What could it be? Both men were dressed normally. But there was something about their skin tone, though it was hard to tell in the semi-darkness. Even people whose differentness was purely physical might tend to turn up here. Here in the bar, here on Polk.

Finally he asked "You from around here?"

"No. From out nuk town." He had already known that. Everyone on Polk Street was from out of town.

"Where from?"

"Um, nuk Czechoslovakia." Huh. They did have accents, but he wouldn't have thought they were central or eastern European accents. He suspected that it was a lie, that they just didn't want to tell where they were really from. He was slightly intrigued.

"What brought you here?"

The man gave a little grunt, a small sigh. "Well, to tell you the truth, where I came uk from, we, they, tended to think we were well, tuk tuk, a little odd. Just a little different from most people around there, that's all. But here in this neighborhood, nobody pay much attentions nuk us. Now, if you'll excuse we."

They got up and walked away. Dwayne looked out the door after them. Yes, there was something about their skin tone, hair, eyes, the way their clothes sat on them, something a little different. Now he was really intrigued, and, leaving his drink not quite finished, left the bar and followed after them, but on the other side of the street. The throng-crowded street. The two walked a block and a half and, coming to the (cheap but not cheap-cheap) Bandling Hotel, went in. Dwayne waited patiently to see which dark window would light up; as soon as he saw, he turned and scurried up stairs to the second floor of the building facing the hotel. He knew it would be open because the sign downstairs of the "painless dentist" upstairs said it would be. Should anyone see him lurking in the upper hall, why, anyone would assume him to be merely a reluctant patient, postponing the inevitable pick and drill.

It was at moments like this that his curiosity (well . . . nosiness) reached the point of a mild sort of voyeurism, and, taking a pair of small binoculars out from under his coat, he peered across into the hotel window. ("Bird-watching," he would have said, if queried. "Have you ever seen a night heron? Shucks! It flew away; I'll go try down at the Marina Green. Bye.") But no one appeared in the hall. The binoculars, which would have shown every feather of a watched bird, under the strong bright light of the hotel room, revealed the two men to look just a bit undefinably odder with their coats off. Still nothing, though, that he could have explained. Except—yes, their skin was just the tiniest bit bluish. Dwayne had worked awhile as an ambulance attendant, and he had a word for this. Or thought he had. "Cyanosis," he murmured. Bad circulation, maybe. Or . . . some sort of liver complaint? But both of them? Well, they were likely brothers, and so no doubt the condition was an hereditary one. Or, at least, congenital.

The two men walked around a bit. One of them drank a glass of water. One of them took off his necktie. And one of them picked up a rather fat, album-like book. And the other—

Damn.

The other pulled down the window-shade.

In the days that followed, Dwayne watched the pair as if they had indeed been birds. Odd birds. Fairly rare or anyway uncommon ones. Night herons? Blue Herons, maybe. This thought made him smile. Dwayne was not often smiley. He watched them coming and he watched them going. He observed where they invariably ate (a semi-health food restaurant where you could get bacon and eggs if you wanted, and / or a large salad with sprouts if you wanted) and at what times they invariably went to eat. He even watched the hotel's employees, and as he knew one of them by sight, slightly cultivated this one's acquaintance. "Let me buy this one, Fred," he said one day.

No great cunning was needed to pump Fred who, for another beer, would have been prepared to reveal the combination to the hotel safe, had he but known it. The two men were indeed brothers. Their names, Fred said, were Boryl and Zorb. They came from Chicago. Chicago, to Fred, might have been a distant archipelago whose inhabitants were even odder than anyone on Polk Street. "Nice quiet people, those brothers in room twenty two," said Fred.

"See you, Fred. I got to go eat."

"Okay," said Fred, with perfect contentment. He was a postgraduate beer-nurser; motto: come day, go day, okay, long as now and then some others pay.

Dwayne did not intend to go eat. He had noticed the brothers Boryl and Zorb heading forward across the street. In two minutes he was in the lobby of the Bandling, casually displaying his props, which he'd been carrying with him for a couple of days. The loaf of bread in the bag printed with the name of the nearby bakery. The book. The bread showed him to be relatively local. The book, to be relatively harmless. Nutty, maybe, but harmless. Nobody challenged him as he made his way to room twenty-two, where, with a deft slide, thrust, and twist, he opened the locked door by means of a plastic ID card which pushed aside the latch.

It was a standard, i.e. horrid, cheap hotel room. Landlord green walls, war-wounded lamp shades, rat-pelt furniture. Twin beds. A single table, scared by cigarette burns and damp glasses, rings accumulated through countless hotel generations: on the table a non-current Chronicle; on the Chronicle, the rather fat album-like book. If one were really from Czechoslovakia, would the room seem richly exotic? From anywhere?

The thought left Dwayne's mind as quickly as it had entered. He opened the book, it was an album. A photograph album, no, they weren't photographs at all: they were cutouts from books produced by the Hare Krishna people. In that case, where were the pictures of Krishna fluting to the cow herd girls? Nowhere. And then he saw that they were, after all, some sort of photographs. So this was what people looked like, back where Boryl and Zorb came from, farther away than Czechoslovakia, or even Chicago. Unlike Boryl and Zorb, with their only faintly blue complexions.

And then it crossed Dwayne's mind that if one came from a place where people looked like this, if you did not look like this, you would indeed be considered, "tuk tuk, slightly odd." Way it went. Was it fair? Look at himself, Dwayne Wombaugh, of Indianola, Indiana. Most guys of course had two testicles. Just because he himself had three, did that make him an oddball? With a sigh, he closed up the album with the pictures of the very bright blue faced people, and went out down into Polk Street again.

~ ~ ~ ~ ~

SAMBO

Avram Davidson & Ethan Davidson

THE CASINO AUDIENCE watched as the muscular young man began to run in circles around the tree. The blue-green Lazarus beam was turned on, and gradually his legs began to disappear. The rest of his body kept moving, without feet, but gradually, that too disappeared.

As the body dissolved, chunks of an elastic-like substance, the shape of long noodles, began to fly into the audience. Every time one of these shapes flew near someone, that one would try to catch it.

When the young man was completely gone, the audience began to throw the elastic-strip substance back into the blue-green Lazarus beam. Gradually the shape of the young man running around the tree came back in. He had a strip of flesh missing under one arm. The audience scrambled around with much good natured banter and the missing strand was finally found under somebody's legs. Sambo's arm was made whole. He stepped running around and bowed to the audience. Great applause.

Sambo sat down to rest, and the set was changed while people sipped the free vodka-mango punch for which the casino was famous.

Now there was a whole clump of trees instead of just one, and a Vlick Screen ("stronger than glass and just as clear") was lowered between the audience and the stage. The tiger had manacled feet, well, actually its feet had been weighted to slow it down, but it could still run fast, and it was hungry. Sambo was given a head start, and he ran fast, for he was literally in a run for his life now. With each lap around the trees, the gap between Sambo and the tiger decreased.

But the Lazarus beam was following the tiger as it ran around and around, so Sambo has only to keep ahead of it until it had disintegrated completely. Gradually the tiger did so, and Sambo paused and caught his breath before turning to bow. Great applause.

The stronger-than-glass-and-just-as-clear Vlick screen was lifted, and the lights concentrated on a transparent trough in front of the stage. The blue-green Lazarus beam was now turned toward the trough, which gradually filled with what eyes and noses identified as melted butter. When it was completely full, men began to bring in tables upon which they set plates of piping-hot pancakes, and an announcement was made that everybody was free to ear. Sambo himself was served the first plate of pancakes.

"That's one hell of a show you put on," said the person from the press to Sambo's manager.

"Yes, we think so," said she.

"Has anything ever gone wrong?"

"Depends on what you mean by—well, yes. One time a woman in the audience got the notion that she just had to kiss Sambo. Well, she got her lips in the Lazarus, the energy beam, you know? And they fused together. She had to have plastic surgery to get them apart." Manager and press-person agreed it served her right.

"What about re-assembling the young Sambo men; do you ever have any trouble with that?"

The manager said, "Oh, no. As long as we have all the pieces, we can do that easily." She put one of the fashionable Cannaby Street simurillos in her mouth.

Some folks in the audience had just made the frequently made discovery that vodka-mango punch mixed very well with melted butter on the pancakes. Laughter in the audience. Great applause.

"I was quite impressed by the way you changed the tigers, well, the tiger, into melted butter at the end," said the press person. "That for real?"

The manager nodded and took the Cannaby Street out of of her mouth. "Oh yes, no slight of hand there. The Lazarus is connected, tuned-in, y'know, to our new Modern Alchemy, y'know, our new MA InterChem computer which, hm, well, it just changes anything into anything else which contains the same chemical interfracts—in this case, calcium, oleo, protein and, well, so on and so on—see?"

The press person said that she saw, and had one last question.

"Where do you get all these tigers? There aren't all that many tigers in the world these days. Aren't exactly plenty of them anymore?"

The manager nodded. "No." she said, "but there are plenty of young men."

~ ~ ~ ~ ~

Ethan Davidson

I wrote this after Avram's death using the notes Avram had left for an unfinished Unhistory.

Unfortunately, much of what we wrote about contemporary Pygmy life is not contemporary anymore. Africa's many civil wars unsettled the Pygmies along with everybody else, and many of them were driven into refugee camps.

This sort of thing tends to happen when you are writing about real, rather than imaginary peoples.

ADVENTURES IN UNHISTORY

THE WAR BETWEEN THE PYGMIES AND THE CRANES

Avram Davidson & Ethan Davidson

HERE COMES HOMER. He walks through western Asia Minor (the eastern part of Greece). He sings, or perhaps he chants, or perhaps he just recites as he plucks his harp or lyre, that guitar of the ancient ages. Now and then he turns his sightless eyes to the wine dark sea. He sings, literally, for his supper, probably a stale piece of bread and a cup of watered wine. If he happens to be allowed into a big man's house on some festival day, he hopes for someone to carve him a thick slice out of the chin of a roasted pork, and he presses home his hope by reciting some lines about just such a scene. Ordinarily, he seldom receives even a fresh piece of bread. And then, too, he must feed whatever lad is guiding him along the unpaved road.

He harps upon the wrath of Achilles, and Nestor's chariot, and Hector dragged 'round the walls of Troy,' and the eagle with a fawn in its talons. And as calmly as he tells his listen-

79

ers that cranes fly south, and that cranes, as they do so, make a great noise, he tells his listeners also that at the end of their far reaching flight, the cranes work bloody murder on the poor Pygmies.

When reading in Homer that the ancient Greeks built a hollow horse and used it to smuggle soldiers, no one is moved to ask why they hadn't built a hollow soldier and used it to smuggle horses. Why, then, when reading in Homer that the cranes waged war upon the Pygmies, am I moved to ask why it wasn't the Pygmies who waged war upon the cranes?

We all know, or anyway we used to know, perhaps it isn't stressed on radio or television (does it sell fudge?), that there was a war between the Trojans and the Greeks. The ancient explanation was that the wife of a Grecian king had run off with a Trojan prince. A modern explanation is that A) the war was over control of the trade routes between the Mediterranean and the Black Sea, or B) there wasn't any such war, just a bunch of old songs and stories that were put together to pass the hours around the house fires when there were no more marshmallows.

One of those old stories, in The Illiad, tells us that the Trojans descended upon the Greeks:

"Like cranes in clamorous lines before the face of heaven, beating away before the winter's gloom and storms, over the streams and oceans, calling to bring a slaughter on the races of small-bodied Pygmy warriors, cranes at dawn descending, beaked in cruel attack."

For the purposes of this Adventure, I am going to assume that the Iliad was composed by Homer, and not by another blind man named Homer who lived in the same place at the same time.

It does, however, seem reasonable to ask if the Pygmies to which he referred were the same sort of Pygmies who now live in the forests of Africa, or if they were another real or mythological race of small-bodied people.

The answer is that there is no reason to doubt that Homer was indeed referring to African Pygmies. Egyptian hieroglyphics report that the ancient Egyptians discovered the Pygmies during a journey to seek the source of the Nile, about 2,500 B.C.E. They were quite impressed by these small people, and even brought one back with them. Later records show that the Egyptians had become fairly knowledgeable about them. The culture of the ancient Greeks, of course, was heavily influenced by the Egyptians.

None of this, however, answers our basic question. We now know that the Pygmies, though small, are not so small as the Greeks seemed to think. Furthermore, they are expert hunters, capable, for example, of killing elephants. And yet it is not, as one would have thought, the Pygmies who are bringing slaughter and death to the cranes. It is the cranes who are bringing slaughter and death to the Pygmies.

Strabo said that the Pygmies are a myth. Aristotle had even earlier said that they were not a myth, though he was aware that some had said that they were. Ovid, during the reign of Augustus, seemed to be writing about everything in the manner of myth. He said that the bird "delights in the blood of the Pygmies." And Juvenal, later yet, during the reign of Trajan and Hadrian, goes Ovid several steps better as to details.

"The Pygmy warrior marches forth with his tiny arms to encounter the swoop and clamorous cloud of the Tracian birds. But soon, no match for his foe, he is snatched up by the savage crane and borne in his crooked talons through the air. If you saw this in our own country, you would shake with laughter. But in that land where the whole populous is only one foot high, though like battles are witnessed every day, no one laughs."

So says Juvenal, Satire XIII. "Shake with laughter," would we, eh Juve? A funny sense of humor, though probably par for the course. Death in the arena, men striving to slaughter one another, men, women and children being fed to lions, dissidents dipped in tar and set alight, always leaves 'em laughing. Ah the pax Romana.

But perhaps more to the point than his, shall we say, sardonic sense of humor is that Juvenal is believed to have spent a number of years exiled, not to Romania like Ovid, but to Egypt. In other words, he was closer to the source of our legend. Do we see signs of this in our account? Well, he says that the Pygmies were armed, and that they fought back, and that much good it did them, too. Does it do us much good to be told that they were only "one foot high?" This seems to take us backwards rather than forwards.

Perhaps more recent descriptions will give us a clue. The Portuguese explorers of the sixteenth and seventeenth centuries described the Pygmies as flying through tree tops, and as having tails. It is easy to see how the stories about the tails might have gotten started, for Pygmies like to wear loin cloths of brown fabric made from beaten bark, and the women, especially, like to leave a long strip of it hanging between their legs. They say that it looks good when they dance.

In any case, it seems obvious that the Portuguese had confused the Pygmies with monkeys, and it seems likely that others before them made the same mistake. Some monkeys are only one foot tall. It is quite plausible that a large predatory bird might have been seen at some point carrying a live monkey, or that a large scavenger bird might have picked up a dead one. Cranes, it is true, eat fish, not monkeys. But when their beaks are closed, one can tell if there is something inside them, but not what that something is. And so the story may have spread.

But if it is possible that the people in our story are really animals, it is also possible that the opposite is true.

The Pygmies of the modern world exist in a symbiotic, relatively peaceful relationship with the other Africans among whom they live. They are hunters and gatherers. Their neighbors are mainly farmers. They trade some of the meat that they catch for some of the food that is grown on the farms. It is true that they also sometimes steal food from these farms, an act which they don't seem to regard as significantly different from gathering food in the forest. But their neighbors, who find them useful, generally tolerate this petty theft.

But the Pygmies whom the Egyptians encountered when they journeyed up the Nile were probably surrounded by Nihlotic tribesmen who were not farmers, but herders of cattle.

Pastoral people often have a reputation for being aggressive, and those on the Nile are no exception. Travelers have reported that the Nuer, for example, are very prone to fighting. They are sensitive, and are easily offended. They are encouraged from early childhood to settle all disputes by fighting, and they value the skills of a fighter as being very important.

Travelers have also noticed other interesting things about the Nihlotic tribes. The Masai, for example, can stand on one leg, with the other tucked behind its knee, for hours. Observers have described their appearance, when in this position, as "stork like."

And about the Shilluk it has been said that a characteristic pose is to stand on one foot and, bending the other, press the sole of the foot against the inner surface of the knee. They will lean upon a spear, which has been stuck into the ground, for hours.

I suggest that, just as the French have been called "frogs", the South Africans "springboks", and the New Zealanders "Kiwis", so either the Nuer, Dinka, Shilluk, or Masai, or some other tribe antecedent to them all, were called "cranes" and that this knowledge simply got lost as the tale traveled from North to South, from continent to continent, and from age to age. It is my theory (and it is really no more than that) that these proto Nihlotics and the Pygmies once lived closer together than they do today, close enough that it would have been possible for the "cranes" to make war upon the Pygmies. Why? Perhaps the Nihlotic herders, who measured their wealth in heads of cattle, were angered by the Pygmies who, as hunter-gatherers, did not understand the concept of a human being owning an animal, and so, may have hunted some of that cattle.

It was said, somewhere, by a scholar in the 20th century, that "we are nearer to the fall of Babylon than the fall of

Babylon was to the founding of Babylon." In like manner, we may say that we are nearer to the time when Homer last told this story than Homer was to the time when this story was first told.

When he was dying, and before death closed his eyes, he lay by the embers of a dying fire, this dying bard who was dying as all men must die. And did he not think, as the cold of death encompassed him, "many men sat silent as I sang my songs."

~ ~ ~ ~ ~

AVRAM DAVIDSON

Carol Carr

This was written for the book Everybody Has Somebody in Heaven: Essential Jewish Tales of the Spirit, by Avram Davidson *(edited by Jack Dann & Grania Davidson Davis, Devora Publishing, 2000)—a collection of Avram's experiences from World War II to his death in 1993.*

IN 1964, A FEW years after I met Avram, I asked him for a favor. He was not grumpy yet, in those days, which was a good thing, for like all my people I am thin-skinned and will carry a grudge to the grave, on my back. I asked Avram if he would mind translating a letter I'd received. It had been sent to me by a cousin in Israel, assuming that I could read Hebrew. As if. I sent Avram a copy of the letter and waited, and pretty soon I received his reply:

"I gamely put aside my two longoverdue [*sic*] novuels [*sic*]," he wrote [notice the deft synthesis of guilt-tripping and innovative spelling] . . . and produced the following:

Dear Carol great peace. I have your letter received. And it has me very happied to hear from you. Thee terribly helping with all possibles. But illegible how thus you be now in Amerika. Israel."

It goes on. So does Avram, and he apologizes for not finishing the translation and not doing a better job of it, and ends with: "Please excuse me a million times; go into a kosher butcher's and buy a lb of meat and ask him to translate for you. Are there no ivory towers anymore?" And then he adds, inexplicably: "I'm not even cooking this week, peanut butter and eggs." Looking at his letters, almost thirty years later, I see uncanny similarities between Avram's prose and Phil Dick's—their off-the-wall humor, temperament, and eccentric brilliance. What can I possibly say about Avram that he didn't say better himself, if only he could read his handwriting. Now and then I'd have the honor of proofreading Avram's stories, for publication in one of Terry Carr's anthologies (Avram bought Terry's first story for *The Magazine of Fantasy & Science Fiction*; later, Terry bought Avram's).

It was a terrifying experience. With most authors, proofreading was a piece of cake—you leave something alone or you change or delete it. Before starting a story of Avram's I'd call my therapist back from vacation, take a long hot bath, and sign up for a linguistics course. When the great day came I'd read one word at a time and then take a nap in order to be refreshed for the next word. You just couldn't be too careful. What looked like a common typo could be, and most likely was, the long-dead future perfect tense of the irregular verb "to fall to one's knees in a cold sweat." And it should not—*must* not—be disturbed.

Avram and I had little relationship to speak of outside of occasional letters, social-type visits, and random meetings at conventions. But we had great flavor together. He often began his letters to me: "Dear Teeny-tiny, eentsy-weentsy, itsy-bitsy, Carolkin," (whomp! that should do wonders for his bearded, dignified image). Since I was none of those things, I adored it. And here is a typical closing:

I cannot write more right now, as my every move is being watched by secret agents from Birobidjan, who are also spreading rumors that I am paranoid. When merely being noid is bad enough. Love, from bubby, only be well.

See what I mean about Phil Dick?

Once Avram visited us with his son, a very young Ethan. They sat close to each other on the couch and spoke in an unknown language that was probably a subdialect used by fathers and sons in Ancient Sumeria. I had no idea what they were saying, but I could tell it was rich, complex, and lit with love.

Years passed. We were in California, he was everywhere. In 1980 he wrote:

Last week I bought some office supplies and slightly overpaid. Today I returned and a person handed me an envelope saying the change was inside. I didn't examine the envelope till I got home, and found that on the envelope, in a corner, as an aide-memoire evidently, someone had penciled, "Little old man with cane." I tottered off to bed at once.

In 1983 my mother died. Avram:

For your pain and sorrow, I am painfully sorry. There is, however, I have noticed, usually, a certain measure of relief. And for whatever relief you feel, feel therein neither pain nor sorrow. Flow with it. Resume the voyage, float, float; and whenever crocodiles appear, whack them on the snout with the paddle.

A Jew, a poet, a Zen grief counselor.

In 1989 Avram wrote ("Dear eentsy-weentsy," etc., still) to ask me if I could find, among Terry's papers, a certain manuscript he'd lost track of. "Now, Carol, it is highly desired that I should have this in order to have something else to neglect."

And he ended one of his last letters to me with this fillip of brazen insouciance: "Well, time to cover the parrot."

Indeed. Sleep well, Avram, and don't forget to whack those crocodiles.

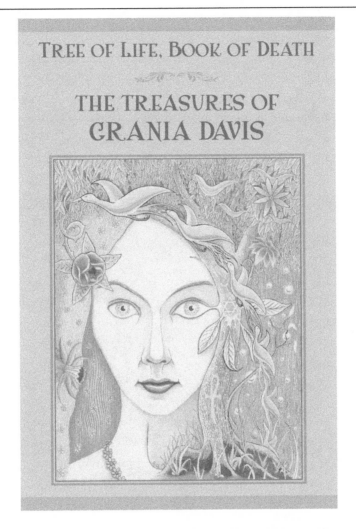

Still available from Surinam Turtle Press & Ramble House

Tree of Life, Book of Death:
The Treasures of Grania Davis

This collection includes **Grania Davis'** short stories and memoirs for those of us who remember the times of the Milford writers. In fifteen stories, some written with her former late husband, Avram Davidson, and one long memoir (which is labeled "not an autobiography") she has chronicled more than just her life—she's written the story of a generation.

ARNTEN OF ULTIMA THULE

Avram Davidson

I

IN THE DARKNESS of his granduncle's medicine hut by the flickerflicker of the faint fire (which the man was allowed to have, grudgingly, and at high tax, for preparing his simple witcheries) the boy recollected the sound of the taptap beats on the tiny witchery-drum and the sight of the mandrakes lifting the lid of their bark box house and coming out to dance by the fire, tossing up their small-small scrannel arms and stamping their tiny-tiny feet to the toom-*toom*, toom-*toom*, toom-*toom*petty-*toom* of the child-sized drum—then dancing backward and closing the lid on themselves as-the last faint pulse beat died away.

A small man, his uncle or granduncle (in those days the boy did not distinguish), with a skill in small witcheries and small magics by which he sustained them. And the boy felt proud of seeing what other boys did not see.

But most of his memories before the breakaway were ill ones.

When he grew big enough to wander from the partly underground medicine hut or the round thatched house where his uncle's sister sat mumbling as she pounded bark or stirred the acorn gruel, the boy learned swiftly enough of how little he had to pride himself in. If you are smaller by far than the smallest of any born in your birth year, if they are smooth of skin and fair of hair and you are dark and your swarthy skin is covered with a nap or bloom of dark hair— are these things to be proud of? If others have fathers and brothers who return from the hunt to be greeted by the singing of their women and if your only family connection with it all is when old uncle or old uncle's sister comes stooping up and waits for a bone or an offal to be tossed as to a dog— is there pride in this?

To be sure, he was quicker of body and sharper of mind than any of his birth year; sharp and quick enough to learn that sharpness and quickness won praise only for others and in him were only to be resented. That magic and witchery produced fear and that fear often produced respect; but that small-scale magic and witchery caused only small fear— suspicion, rather—and hardly ever respect at all. For fear and fears hung over the town like the smoke from the great central fire on lowering days. Fear that someone was working a witchery, fear of the wild ones of the woods, fear of the king and the tax-gathers, fear of known magic and of unknown even more. And the boy who was small and sharp and dark and shaggy produced an effect of strangeness which was like the subtle smell of fear—but was not strong enough to ward off the hates and wraths which this caused—and besides— and besides . . .

The affair of the great roan mammont, the rogue mammont, fear of fears and terror of terrors, brought all things to a head; but before that, long-long before that day of blood and death, that day of the hill-that-moved, the trees-that-walk, serpent-snout and spear-teeth and all the other names used when one dares not use the real name: *mammont*; long before then, when he was very small, there was the token.

The token hung on a thong from a peg in a post in his grandmother's hut. For a while it was above his head and he reached for it often while the old one squatted, mumbling, in the sun of the door-front. He could not remember the first time he actually reached it, standing on a stool (probably), but he had a clear recollection of one day scanning it and seeing it and recognizing it. It was carved of wood, roughly but forcefully, in the form of a bear. It had the bear's head and one tooth clearly in the crude snout; it had the bear's paws and legs. But the legs ended in the feet of a man.

~ ~ ~ ~ ~

PERHAPS at that time he had not recognized this strangeness; he had certainly never seen a bear, for it was not till later that Tall Roke brought in the cub which was partly petted and partly tortured until it was abruptly killed and eaten. Likely at that child-time he did not know that a bear has bear's feet and that although they resemble a man's, yet they are not. Nor was it yet clear to him how subtly manlike the carving was.

But he had the clear recollection of scanning it that one day and becoming aware that the old woman, granduncle's sister and his own grandmother, had come in and was staring at him, on her blear and withered face a look odd even for her on whom odd looks were common. A look of fear and love and awe and horror.

Sensing that she was in what was for her a lucid mood, he asked as he pointed, "This—what?"

And she, promptly and matter-of-factly, said, "Your father." And as promptly thrust awry her snaggle-snarl hair and screamed and rolled her rheumy eyes and tore open the bosom of her bark-cloth dress and beat and scratched her withered dugs and wailed and howled and beat her head upon the earthen floor. "Hinna!" she screamed. "Hinna! Hinna!" and, "Hinna-tenna!"

Such fits and antics were not so rare as to alarm the boy—for all he knew, all grandmothers behaved so—just as, for all he knew, all fathers were carved of wood and hung on leather thongs from posts. But this fit was uncommon severe and he appreciated, in fact, he rather enjoyed the new aspects of it, as he might have enjoyed a new grip noted in a dog-fight.

Hinna. So the old man sometimes addressed the old woman. Sometimes the old woman said it as she pointed out the small blue flowers of a plant occasionally brought back with other herbs and roots or leaves and barks from the woods by the old man. So: Hinna was the old woman and hinna was a flower, but he knew that this old woman was not thrown into a fit in order to mention either; he did not know *how* he knew and wondered, mildly, that he knew at all. Logic was here working scarcely above the level of intuition.

The old woman shrieked and babbled of something which was "Woe!" but mostly her words were strange and, *"Hinna-tenna!"* she screamed. And, *"Arn't! Arn't Arn't!"*

And then the old uncle was kneeling beside her, soothing her, calming her, arranging her tattered dress of pounded bark-lining, carrying her—at last, when her voice was a mere croon or drone—to the worn-almost-hairless half of deerhide which covered her grass bed. And the old man got up and seemed at a loss as he looked at the boy. Who sensed and instantly seized an opportunity.

Pointing to the token on the thong, "My father," he said.

"Yes," said the old man, unsurprised. Then he winced.

What made the boy say what he next said, still pointing? No knowing—unless it was unrealized awareness of a connection between strange things enclosed in a space of time—such as this moment which had just passed, or perhaps still was passing.

Pointing to the token he said. "Arn't. Arn't."

"Arn," his uncle said, absentminded correction in his tone.

So. *Arn* was the token which was the bear which was his father and his father had somehow thrown the old woman into a fit in which *Arn't* was somehow different. And what else was in the fit which was familiar yet different—for something was.

Ah.

"Tenna," the boy said; immediately correcting himself: *"Hinna-tenna."*

Without so much as a sigh and in the same flat, abstracted voice in which he would explain to a visitor at the medicine hut the care and feeding of mandrakes or the price of a charm or the manner of a charm (other men whose work was witchery had the better sense to sink their voices and roll their eyes and make at least a few fearful gestures and whisper at least a few words in a doleful whisper, lips to ear. Other witcherers commanded higher prices, too, got amber-grains and goodly pelts, were not content with bones and offals) his granduncle said to him, "Hinna is the cornflower and is also my sister's name. Your grandmother. Was her daughter's

name. Your mother. *Tenna* is a word in the Old Tongue, now
archaic, used chiefly for witchery. Spoken sometimes by
such relics as myself and sister. Tenna means 'daughter.' *Arn*
in the older tongue is 'bear.' So, now I consider it *'Arn't'*
may be applied to the token, for my sister's daughter said she
had it of the bear. As she said, too, she had you. But she was
never right in her wits after that and grew worse and we
found her drowned."

After a moment he nodded once or twice and left the
house without more word, confident, apparently, that he had
said everything there was to be said. As, perhaps, he had.

~ ~ ~ ~ ~

THE boy realized, growing older, that often he himself saw
sequences and connections where other boys saw none. But
just as he could see logic and they not, just so things that
seemed sensible to them were senseless and unpredictable to
him. More than once he had been stoned away from following hunters, yet today he had been asked—not allowed,
asked—"Come, honey-dripper, bring us good luck!" And
here he was with the rest of them in the high grass and the
sun hot upon the earth and on them all so that he could smell
it and them and the grass and other things not even seen.

Honey-dripper, with a guffaw. It was a name for him.
Comb-robber was another. Both meant *bear*, who stole the
honeycomb from the honey tree and ate it, dripping its rich-
ness, grubs and wax and all. But *comb-robber*, applied to
him, was merely an ill-name. *Honey-dripper* was less so,
was a laughing term, and—somehow—referred not exclu-
sively to the bear but also had something to do with men and
the things men had with women. Tall Roke it was who'd said
him this name this day and asked him to come; and Tall
Roke it was, when another had looked black and muttered,
who had briskly and blithely answered, "What? For that
some rough fellow tumbled his mad mother and gamed her,
saying, 'I'm a bear!' What? A bigger fool than she or you I'd
be to think the kid an ill-bringer for that. Ah no, but that his

old uncle's witchery had maybe rubbed off on him a bit, and then a-smells as wild as any beasty and so may cover our own manstinks—"

But as yet the boy could not smell the wild white horses they were hunting—the swift, mane-tossing, clever-cunning, clever-mad, mad-eyed, red-eyed, wild-eyed, wild, white horses—whom no man's mind or hand had ever yet thought to tame. Three days since, some village stripling, gaming about in the meadows, had found a colt with its leg broken in a mole hole, had swiftly (but, be sure, not without a swifter, fearful lookabout) cut its throat and borne it home. Perhaps one of its marrowbones was still stewing in a pot of spelt; the rest had sure been eaten. But the clever-mad horses of the herd had tracked the lostling down to its place of injury, had seen the blood, had traced the drips of blood as far to the village as even their mad courage cared to go. Since then they had been waging war: trampling crops, attacking cultivators and wanderers with hooves and teeth. So now the menfolk were carrying the war unto the horsefolk.

Time was when only the poorest of the poor would have had stone or bone for his weapons. All else had had iron— had even had arrow or spear-heads to spare, in case of break-age before a wandernain (some called them "shamblenain," but not to their faces) would come trading new irons for old: amber and peltries their fee: taking the broken points with them back to strange and distant Nainland to mend upon their witchery-forge, an art which only the nains had. As for bronze, that was only a memory, bronze had long since died of the green-sickness. As yet, out here, the deadly rust was moving slowly, but move it did; something was deadly wrong with iron, and no nains came; grim was the mood of the distant king, and—

"Hist, now," said Tall Roke. "Mind the plan, now. Drive away the young stallions and the mares with stones, the colts will follow—cut off the great stallion, and whilst we three engage him from in front, you two cut his tendons from be-hind." The great stallion, with hamstrings severed on his hind legs, would go down and never rise. Deprived of leader, the other steeds would flee.

Tall Roke hawked and spat and grunted. He needed not to point. They had come to the edge of the escarpment and in the near distance of the wide, shallow valley, they saw the horses like wee white clouds, floating in the blue-green sky of grass. For a moment they gazed, the five or six full men, the twice that many striplings and the boy who had no name. Then they spread out widely and began the slow and cautious descent from the rim. Slow, for there was no swift going down that uncertain slope; cautious, because they dared not give alarm to the horse herd.

The boy felt for the pouch with the stones in it. The touch was reassuring. Nothing else was. His first hunt. His heart pounding. It had been agreed that any needed signaling would take the form of a ground squirrel's whistling, as this would (at most) arouse the hunger of no creature larger than a fox or hawk. Tentatively the boy formed his mouth to make such a signal. But he never made it. The while he had been keeping a sort of sketch of things in his head. Yonder was the sun. The cliff directly behind. The wind, so. To the right must be the horse herd. A little left of straight ahead were, though now not seen, a clump of thick-boled trees. Beyond that, a low hillock of rusty scrub. A brook. A wallow.

~ ~ ~ ~ ~

ALARM, alarm rose so swift in his chest that it choked his breath. Something was wrong. Everything was wrong. He had gone the wrong way—or—for he was much too close to the hillock, he could see it now, he could not see the trees, which meant—and then came the whistle, and the whistle was to have come from Tall Roke and Tall Roke should be *that* way and the whistle was over *this* way— Vertigo took him, he was on both knees and one hand. Earthshake? For the hillock moved and his eyes fled from it and his eyes saw trees walking and someone screamed and screamed—it was not him, then it was him as it was many others, for by now all knew it was *the hill-that-moves, the trees-that-walk*, all of them could see the *serpent snout* that rose up huge and hairy and drank the wind, all could see the flash of *spear teeth*, all could hear the horrid trumpet scream of the *mammont! mammont! mammont!* as its tree-huge legs shook the grassy ground in its terrible charge, its trunk sweeping down the grass before it as a scythe, bloody scythe, bloody grass, bloody spears, bloody teeth—

Fear and failing flesh and yet senses still undimmed enough to hear Tall Roke's voice full strong as he shouted, "Hold to the plan! Axe men to the rear whilst I engage to the front—" *I* and not *we*, he did not trust to any others' courage to face the huge red mammont from the front, but still had hopes that some might brave the great beast's hind legs to strike at the lower tendons. Onward the mammoth beast had come, fast, fast, but faster yet ran Tall Roke, passing it—so swift he might have escaped, had he run in another direction, had such been his intent—passing it, running backward before it, turning it, darting back and away from it, shouting and feinting his spear at it—"Strike! Strike!" he shouted—

But no one was there to strike. No one was there but Tall Roke. One man. One boy. Who shrieked with all the fury of his unformed voice and cast his stones with all the power of his unformed arms. For one fell moment the mammont wavered, rage-reddened eyes darting from man to boy.

"Ankles! Ankles! Ah! Strike! Ankles!" hoarsely but still hopefully: Tall Roke's voice. But no one struck. And the one man's spear hung in the air, it seemed not so much that he had cast it at the mammont as that the mammont had hurled itself upon the airborne spear: it lanced the line of the great face from tusk-socket to eye-socket: the mammont screamed its pain and rage: again the spear hung in the air: and now— and this was so puzzling—Tall Roke himself hung in the air, his fair hair all in a mist about his face—the python trunk seemed to rise slowly, slowly, slowly, and to descend slowly—slowly, slowly, and to wrap itself so slowly gently lovingly about the man's neck.

~ ~ ~ ~ ~

THERE were flowers in the meadow and bees in the air and then there was a dripping comb of honey and he thrust his paws first into the comb and then into his mouth and its taste was of gold and sweet and strong and delightful beyond the taste of any food tasted before and when it was quite quite gone he licked his paws and he licked the grass it had dripped on and then he went scampering off to where the bushes hung heavy with the full ripe berries and he ate his wonder full of them and

~ ~ ~ ~ ~

THREE of them returned alive to the village and Tall Roke was found alive (though only barely) where the mammont had tossed and gored him but, unaccountably, not trampled him as it had the others. But he, too, was soon dead. Another's head was found in the branches of a tree. Something that was probably his body, for it could be nothing else, was smeared nearby.

The horses had vanished.

That the great roan mammont was a rogue, all agreed. Only a rogue would travel alone, and there was no sign at all of any other mammont—and, for that matter, of that one himself—any more.

At first no one in the village said anything but, *It has happened.* Since the starting of the red-rustsickness of all iron and the increasing wrath of the distant and once indifferent king, since the nains had ceased to visit and the tax exactions had begun to increase, rumors faint as whispers and whispers loud as shouts had been spreading, spreading, spreading. Some great calamity impended. And now it had come. It had happened.

Next in the village they began to ask, *How did it happen?*

By this time the boy thought he knew. And there was one other who, he thought, also thought he knew. And that meant there was a third who certainly knew.

The name of the second was Corm, a lad perhaps a year or two older, eyes gray rather than the common blue, hair not blond and curling but brown and lank, sallow of skin; his father was one of the three subchiefs of the townlet. If Corm had not given the boy many good words, that was nothing, no one did that; but he had never given any ill ones at all. The third was a whey-faced, slack-mouthed, slack-limbed shambelton, with an almost perpetual eruption about the mouth at which he ever picked and which generally bled: a liar and bully and boor, yet well connected—that is, connected to families of some small importance who, by talking loud and often and big, made that small seem greater.

It was one of those moments which seem to have been a part of the center of all things, lying in wait from the beginning. No hint of it before. Old Hinna's grandson standing idly watching. Whey-face shambling along. The boy looking at him. Looking up to see Corm watching Whey-face as well. His eyes meeting Corm's. Instantly, as though spoken words had passed between them: *It was Whey-face who gave that first, wrong whistle, which would have been done right if Tall Roke had done it at the right time if it should have been done at all; it came from where Whey-face was, and only he would have been fool enough, coward enough to have done it, done it in coward-fool hopes of a reassuring return of it: it was that whistle, ill-done, which roused the mammont—in another moment Tall Roke would have seen it and managed to get us all safe away somehow, but—*

Still that same second. Wheyface looking up as though called, catching their glance, understanding, flushing, paling, and at once reacting in his coward way—not coward-foolish this time but coward-cunning. Pointing at the boy, shouting at the boy, attracting instantly every eye and mind voicing the unvoiced and making clamor become instant fact: "It was *him! He* brought the ill-fate, *he* brought the mammont there! The bear's bastard with the bear-stink on him! Bear's bastard! Nain's get! Made the mammont come! Curse-bringer! Shag-skin! Killed our men and boys! *Him! Him! Him!*" And, stooping, he snatched up a piece of dried filth, ran and flung it.

Then sticks, then stones. Next would-be arrows, axes, spears. No need to inquire, discuss, reason, weigh-instant, heart-warming hatred was quick, easy. *"Bear's bastard! Curse-bringer! Men killed! Bear-stink!"* The mammont was gone, the boy remained. He saw Corm's mouth open but neither he nor any heard Corm's word, drowned out in the bull-voiced clamor of all of Whey-face's kith and kin, believing or not believing, belief beside the point, the point: Ours. Support him. Shout loud. Throw something.

The boy ran. Terror runs swifter than rage follows. Boys can go where big men cannot—holes, hollows, runways, dogpaths, shinny up slender trees and drop over palings. There was his old uncle crouching by his slender fire. It was an instant. His grandmother's hut. A packet thrust into his hands, the bark bag with the small victuals the old man took with him when he hunted herbs. A hide lifted up to show an opening the boy had never seen before. A burrow, wide enough for him. A patch of light. The village palisades behind him. An echoing that might have been the clamor of the mob. That might have been the beating of his blood. Something clutched in his other hand. He ran. He ran.

II

"GO, ARNTEN. FIND your father," the old uncle had said as he
lifted the hide-flap. As it fell and all was dark, the boy heard
him say, "It is time." Then nothing but a faint moment of one
of the old man's chantings. *Arnten*. The word lodged like a
grub in a honeycomb cell. *Arnten*. But there was no sign, yet.
A faint thought: *it is my name*. No time for further thought.
Arnten. His name. That and escape. For now, enough. A life.
A name.

In the woods, however, nothing was now asking his name.
With a knowledge deeper than thought he avoided the hard-
trodden dust of the common path and sank into the thicket
like a snake. Behind, he heard the clamor and shouting descend into a single sound on a single note and stay there, like
the noise of a swarm of bees hovering and *mrumming* its one
dull note forever. Somehow it sounded infinitely more men-
acing than any cluster of mere words. Presently the hum-
ming-*mrumming* grew louder. Then loud. The ear-pressed
earth echoed like a drumhead. The echo filled the ear and air.
Suddenly it was gone and he, Arnten, realized that it had
gone a time ago and that he was alone and that if any were
still seeking him, they were not doing it here.

Slowly he rose up in the thicket like a mist. He gained the
path. He snuffed up the breeze. He listened. He was gone.

~ ~ ~ ~ ~

A BIRD sang twit-twit-*twit* on a branch. A ground squirrel
hopped and scampered, scampered and hopped, vanished
from view. There was a smell of wetness, of damp earth and
the scent of the sweet green breath of plants. Arnten knew
that there were times to look up and times to look down and
times to look straight ahead. He saw the bush, he saw
through the bush and, a long, long way beyond the bush he
saw the boles of several trees but nothing in between. Softly,
gently, he pushed the shrubby branches aside. For a moment
he paused, holding his breath, listening. There was not, had

not been for long, sounds of mob or pack or crowd. There had been no man sounds at all, save for his own. It was improbable that any enemy of his own blood was near. It was not impossible.

But he heard no new noise. Only the faint patter of the ground squirrel. Only the same twit-twit-*twit* of the bird on the branch.

He slipped past the handful of branches and let them make their own return to their natural positions, only restraining them enough so that they should close without sound. He went on a bit and then he stopped and considered, there in the cool green corridor which for now meant safety. It had been used enough to create a trail, but little enough to allow the bush's growing to obscure the entrance. Perhaps small and dainty deer slipped along this tunnel through the trees. They would not mind sharing it with him. Or perhaps white tiger, dire wolf, snowy leopard, used it in quest of the same small dainty deer. This thought contracted and shook his limbs in a long shudder. He felt and saw the nap of hairs quiver upon his skin and stand up from the fearful flesh.

His mind leaped from thought to thought as a spark of fire leaps from one twig to another. Another boy, conceiving the same thought, might find his mind working *thought of danger—beast equals danger—beast equals panic—run for your life*, without even realizing the process. But his own mind worked *thought of danger—beast equals* think *about danger—beast*. And he stopped and thought.

The thought is not the thing.

And the thought told him that the thing, the great ones among the danger-beasts, were seldom if ever to be found in this part of Thule at this season of the year; they were to be found (or rather, avoided) farther to the north, where men had less thinned out the game on which they chiefly preyed; winter snows, in which the hooved beasts would flounder and be more easily tracked and trapped and killed, might indeed bring the great killers down.

But then again might not.

He felt the drum within his bosom slow its clamor and then its beats receded to their normal slow strokes, below the threshhold of perception. He began to go on, but the trail was narrow and something caught upon a branch and held him. He looked down and saw he was still carrying without awareness the two things hastily taken in his flight from town. The bark bag of food, the bear-token upon its leathern thong. It was this last he now had to disengage. It seemed somehow as natural to hang it around his neck as to loop the grass cord of the food wallet from shoulder to hip. So. He had no weapon but he had food, itself a sort of weapon—was not hunger the chief enemy? He had a potency in the form of the bear carving, a token of whoever his father was—a father contained in a piece of wood on a thong was better than no father at all. *Find your father, Arnten.* What did he know of how or where? Either his father was or was not a bear. If not, then he knew and could know nothing. If so—then what? Where were bears? Anywhere, manywhere, where there were trees and streams. So. Avoid the grasslands, the great meadows. But he would have done so in any case. There was the game he could not take, there would be the great beasts, the danger-beasts he could not forfend.

Therefore, the forest. A tree creaked. It seemed a Yes.

~ ~ ~ ~ ~

WHEN the balls of boiled millet and scraps of dried meat and fish were gone from his bark bag he went a while without and he hungered. Then there were berries and plants his old herb-uncle had shown him. He ate walking and he slept little. He seemed to need less of either. If the path forked and one branch inclined toward the plains of danger, he took the other. If there was still a choice and a question, he held the token in his hands and pointed it between the paths. It moved. Sometimes slowly, slightly. But it moved. It had one day not yet stopped moving when he felt the eyes upon him and looked up. They were great, glowing, amber eyes—

intelligent eyes, but far too strange to be the eyes of any man. Nor were they.

The figure was squat of body and shag of skin, with a brown main of hair upon scalp and broad face. The extraordinarily long arms were folded across the extraordinarily thick chest. A kilt of soft leather girdled the loins. Short were the powerful legs. Over arms, hands and chest and belly the long brown hair grew thickly. The boy found himself looking at his own body and limbs. Instantly, several thoughts—and one of them as an almost instant surprise: *I am not afraid!* And, another—

"Nay, boy." The voice was strange in more than being unknown. It had odd tones and echoes, the final vowels nasalized so that almost they sounded as *nay'n, boy'n.* "Nay, boy. It's isn't me nurr any we who's is fathered ye 'n given 'e them warm hairs upon yurr's skin." So acutely did the strange one discern his thoughts. And spoke a few words of no understanding, at first, to the boy—whose ear sped back and caught on a word he knew.

"*Arn't.*"

He said, "The bear—"

Something flashed golden in the amber eyes. More strange words. Then— "Ye dow int speak en witchery words—hey'n?" Arnten shook his head. "Nay," murmured the stranger. Almost, it was "Ngayng." He said, "We speak it ever 't'the forge. Ye must's ever speak en 't' Th' Old Tongue t'iron, furr iron 't's a witchery thing. So we speak en it furr habit, ef we dow int think not to—"

"You said—'*Arn't*'—"

"Eh. We speak 's'en it, too, 't'the bear, furr the bear dow be a witchery-beast. All creaturr dow die, but the bear dow come alive agains. And the Star Bear dow gived we-folk the first fire." The glowing eyes fixed his own. The odd voice, strong and strange, but devoid of harm for him, went on. "En all of Thule's the wurrd gone round, '*When the wolf dow meet the bear: beware.*' " There seemed something expectant in his tone, something expectant in his look.

But look and tone alike meant nothing to the boy, who said, as though thinking aloud, "A nain." The nain stopped his head and his shoulders. And the boy said, "Arnten, I am Arnten." And this time the nain stooped his entire thick body to the waist.

Then, straightening, he extended an arm so long that its fingers almost touched Arnten's chest. "We know en what place 't' is." The boy's eyes followed and saw the thick and hairy fingers of the thick and hairy hand were pointing not to his body but to the token slung upon it.

"Where? It is *here*."

The nain grunted, held up a hand straight from the wrist in the nain sign of negation. "Not this. Th' other this. Th'— th'—" He struggled to express himself, his manner rather like that of a man seeking a paraphrase for a thing he does not care to name precisely. "Th' *other* this. *That!*"

And he turned and walked away.

Arnten followed.

~ ~ ~ ~ ~

AFTER a full seven-days' walk they came to it. The place was more of a hole or cleft than a cave, but it was dry. Part of the ceiling had fallen in; boulders littered the floor. The nain without hesitating or pausing put his chest against the largest and wound long arms around it. He moved the stone up and over and then back. "Take 't' up," he said. " 'T's not furr we to touch." *It*, clearly, was not the rock. A moment passed, in the dim light before Arnten saw *it*. For a moment he thought it was a piece of wood. Then, more by intuition than lineal recognition, he knew that what he saw on the ground where the rock had been was a witchery-bundle.'

That.

It was perhaps the size of his forearm and, with his forearm, after he had taken it outside in the sunlight, he wiped at the dusty hide covering. It was certainly a witchery-bundle. There were witchery signs upon it, some clear, some dim, some familiar, some unknown. Largest and most deeply etched were the sun and the bear. The bear was almost certainly a replica of the one he wore. Or—was it the other way around? "The sun," he said.

"Eh'ng," the nain agreed. "The sun and the bear, they go together. For the sun dies and 't comes alive again. And the bear dow die and dow come alive again. The sun give fire and the bear, too. Eh'ng," he said, after a moment, eyeing the hide-covered bundle, and musing. "How many snowtimes? Two hands? Surely two. But three? Surely not three. Bear, he told a-we, Here dow be my token. Here dow by my," the nain gestured, "*that*. Bear telled: 'Look for it. If you see him, manchild-bearchild—if you see my token on'-t'him; show him where.' And we say'd him, Eh'ng-ah, Bear."

It was mystery, but it was good mystery. Witchery, but he could not think it any but good witchery. It was a good moment. Why, then, did the flood of bad memory rise up in his mind, come spilling out of his mouth? "They stoned me. They pelted me with filth. They called me *nain's get* and *bear's bastard* and they tried to kill me."

The nain's amber-colored eyes glowed and darkened and in level sunlight glowed like a beast's in the night, glowed red, glowed like an amber in the nighttime fire.

Words like distant thunder rolled in his vast chest and rumbled in his wide throat.

"Wolf's lice! Accursed smoothskins!" He spoke at last in the common tongue and continued to do so, though occasionally dropping into naintalk or the archaic language of witchery. "If it were not for us and our iron they would still be eating of grubs and lizards and roots. And what will they do now, as iron dies? Is there one of them, a single one even, with cunning and courage enough to feed the wizards? Their king, ah, he might have, when he was young, but he's gotten old now, he's gotten half-mad now, he looks in the wrong direction, he afflicts where no affliction can help, the wind blows cruel hard from the north but he thinks it blows from the south! A nain's life is that it's worth to try to persuade him—if a nain wished it. As for the rest of the slim race—"

He caught his breath, part in a sigh, part in a sob. The fiery glow in his eyes began to die away.

"Nay, I'll say no more as regards that race and blood, 'tis partly yours. They may deny it, may deny you—you may wish to deny it and them. But the blood cannot be denied. Nay, nay. The blood cannot be denied." Abruptly, gesturing to the bundle, the nain said, "Open it then."

The outer covering had been tied tight with sinews, but his probing fingers found one loose enough to allow his teeth purchase. He gnawed, felt the fibers give way—give until his teeth met with a click. Quickly his fingernails pulled the thread, tugged it from pierced hole, from the next and next. Some sort of dried membrane—the bladder, perhaps, of a large animal—was inside the outer covering, bound about with bark cord which did not long resist attack. Inside was a long pouch with a drawstring tied in tassels. Carefully he unfastened this, carefully he laid out the contents on the outer wrappings.

First, by size alone, was a knife in a sheath of horn and leather, with a good bone handle carved in the same likeness of a bear. It was entirely unaffected by the iron-rot. It was a good knife.

There was also a dried and withered beechnut.

There was also a greenstone.

There was also a bear's claw.

There was also, bent and doubled, but not yet broken, a river-reed. There was nothing else. He looked up to ask about these, but the nain was gone.

~ ~ ~ ~ ~

EVERY man had a witchery-bundle; even children devised them in imitation of their elders. Some had richly adorned ones, the contents bought of high-priced witcherers for nuggets of amber and pelts of marten, sable, ermine, white tigers, snow leopards. Some had but meager pouches containing perhaps a single item—a bone, a dried this-or-that, a something seen in a dream and sought for and found. A tooth pried from a dry skull. A fragment of something said to be a thunderstone.

Some had inherited.

So had he.

The knife alone would at any time have been deemed a good inheritage, the more so now that good iron was hard to find and harder to keep. The more so for the circumstances of its hiding and finding. But what did the other mean? A bear claw, now that was easy to understand. But the reed? The greenstone? *Arnten, find your father.* Had he found him? Not yet. But now, having found this much, might he not find a source? For as long—no, longer—than he himself had lived, the nains had not seen his father. He might be dead. He might be far away. He might be neither. He might be alive and very near.

Arnten carefully restored the magic items to their pouch—except for the knife, which he slung about his waist—and started off. Excitement and happiness had made him heedless and when he heard the low-voiced song in the clearing he had no thought but to see who was singing it.

It was one of the Painted Men, that was at once obvious—one of the Painted Men whom it was death to see unpainted. By greatest good fortune, though, he had just finished painting himself, however—and what a curious pattern his skin did present! Almost hideous. Not till the man, still humming his witchery-song, lifted his brush and dipped it in a tiny pot did Arnten realize, cold with horror, that what he was seeing was the man's naked skin!—that he had only then begun.

The Painted (or unPainted) Man swung about, panting with shame and rage. Arnten felt the club's first blow.

III

THE OLD NAIN stood stolidly where the uneasy soldiers had
bade him stand. He could without great effort have broken
the ribs of all of them and the necks of most before any of
them could stop him —and perhaps it was this that made
them uneasy. But perhaps not. The king's camp and court
was an uneasy place in general these days—not that the rest
of Thule lay at much ease either. Slots of sunlight came
through the smoke hole in the top of the great tent. The king
sat back on a pelt-piled bench and the nain thought it seemed
they lied who said the king was age-wasted. Indeed, as the
Orfas sat there, glaring, hands clenched upon his knees, he
seemed all too vigorous. Within himself the old nain sighed a
slight sigh. Only to the extent that the smoothskins were unpredictable were they predictable at all. Ah, eh. Seasons
come and seasons go and ever the race of nains would remain upon the earth. Meanwhile, one endured. Heat, cold,
toil, hunger, thirst, a savage beast, an unwise king.

A witchery queen.

The soldiers, fumbling and breathing their unhappiness,
finished shackling the old nain's horsehide fetters to one of
the roof posts, were angrily waved outside, almost stumbled
over each other in their eagerness to obey.

For a long moment the king continued to glare. Then he
said, slowly and with effort, but quite correctly, "Uur-
tenokh-tenokh-guur."

So, this was something. At least the king remembered the
nain's proper name. Or had learned it. A small courtesy, perhaps. But a courtesy. He would return it. "Orfas," he said.

The king's head snapped up with a jerk. He was not angered, he was not pleased, his attention had been called to
something forgotten. Probably it had been long since he had
been called by his own name in The Old Tongue, called anything (perhaps) save King or Great Bull Mammont or some
other lickleg flattery such as the smoothskins used. The old
nain almost without thinking essayed more syllables in the
witchery language, but the king's swift gesture cut him off.

"My store of that speech has rusted in my mind," Orfas said, "as has my story of the iron you have cursed." His head shifted, his eyes flashed. "*Why* have you cursed it?"

"We have not. Do you curse your kingdom?"

"You are the High Smith of the nains. I have not had you brought here to bandy questions with me."

"You had not brought me here at all, had I not thought you would keep your word."

Bluff and bluster. What? Not kept his word? How?

"You said I would not be bound."

A false and further look of outraged pride, falling into one of faint regret and helplessness at having been stupidly misunderstood. "I said that you would not be bound with iron."

"Is it by such cunning shift of words that you hope to command either my respect or my assistance?" The king flushed, either in affront or from some vestigial sense of shame. "Do you think me an owl or a bat, unable to see in daylight? I see that none of your captives are bound in iron. It is not out of any honor that I have been bound in thongs of skin, but because you no longer trust iron." It was a statement, not a question, it went home. The king looked aside, for a moment at a loss. "I will give you an advice—" The king sat up. "Sea-cow's skin is tougher by far and far less risky to hunt."

The king growled and moved on his bench. Then he came forward and, stooping, loosed the High Smith's bounds. "It is well," the old nain said aloud. In his mind he said that in the brighter light the Orfas looked his full age indeed. Gray streaked the once yellow hair, now scanted. The smoothskin was no longer quite so smooth of skin at all: here wrinkled, there slack, elsewhere puffed with fat where not hollowed. It was nonetheless well, this act. Uur-tenokh-tenokh-guur sat and the king sat before him. Would he eat?—Would he drink? the king asked. The nain grunted, held his hand up. No. A silence fell. "Listen," said the king at last. "What will you nains do when the barbar-folk invade?"

"I do not know that they will invade. I do not believe that they will invade. Why do you think so?"

The king restrained himself. Beneath his shag eyebrows his eyes looked at the nain like the waters of a wintry sea. "Why should they not invade? Are we now known to them as the source of great wealth? Amber and ivory and peltry— do they not value these things? Is there not a proverb, *When the prey stumbles, the hunter sharpens his knife*? They will invade to gain our wealth; they will invade because without iron, good iron for weapons, we are weak before them; they will invade because I tell you they intend to invade and it is in order to strengthen themselves by weakening us that they have cursed our iron—"

The old nain wheezed in the way that nains have and he said, "So now it is the barbar-folk who have cursed iron. And not the nains."

Slant-glanced, Orfas looked at him. "All the witchery of iron is yours and you have kept it yours and we have suffered you to keep it yours. Besides the one kept by treaty at my court, there has been no forge outside of Nainland. If any man had a broken spear or plowpoint, he had to wait in hopes of a wandernain coming by with unbroken spear or plowpoint to trade him old for new plus a goodly gift— Nay, High Smith. I never begrudged the nainfee, myself paying highest of all. If this is at the bottom of all, let it be said the nainfee will be raised, let it be doubled, tripled—"

"It is not we."

The king's teeth clenched upon a strand of beard he had thrust into his mouth. "What has ever happened to iron without the nains' causing it to happen?"

"This is a new thing, King. Had we not asked you long before you asked we?"

The king's hand made a movement, the king's face made a movement. The king was not in an instant -persuaded. "You asked in order to cover yourself. But you have not covered yourself. Do you not know that *the king's ears are the longest ears in Thule*? I hear all things and I can, from what I hear, reckon all things. Thus it is that I know that iron is accursed, that the nainfolk have cursed it—at whose behest and for what purpose? Your silence is useless. Speak, then."

The old nain sighed.

"If you hear all things, then already you have heard of what the nains say among the nains in Nainland, namely that it is doubtless a device of the neglected wizards of Wizard-land in order to ensure that they do not remain neglected: this curse, the death of iron. And if from what you hear you can reckon all things, then you can reckon what needs be done."

Now it was the king who sighed.

"You speak to me as though we were two old women pounding bark. You will speak differently if I come upon Nainland with all my men."

The old High Smith shook his massive head. "It is all one, if you come upon Nainland with all your men or with but one or none of your men. The forges of Nainland are cold, Orfas. The forges of Nainland are cold."

~ ~ ~ ~ ~

As HE stepped from the outer to the inner of the two rooms in which he was to be lodged—or confined—he saw three great white flowers lying together upon a mat. He stopped still.

"I thought you might remember," a voice said. "I thought it might please you."

"Dame, I do remember," the old nain said. "And I am pleased."

He touched without bending down the flowers with his fingers. The blooms were scentless, but the room contained the scent of some that had never blossomed in the northern land of Thule. He had heard of the tiny horns and small flasks carven in strange designs upon strange stone, which contained the odorous essences of plants for which Thule had no name, delivered at intervals in trading vessels for great price and for the anointing and the pleasure of the Orfas Queen. He turned.

"Your face told me that you had never seen them before and that they pleased you; so I gave them to you, the three of them, and presently you gave me these—" She took from her broad bejewled belt the ivory case containing the three small things so carefully wrought: dirk and spoon and comb. "Only see," she said, sorrowfully. The red-rotted metal crumbled at her slight finger touch. "Can you not effect a cure?"

His broad stern face relaxed into something much like sorrow, he held both his hands straight up at the wrists. "They are so small," he said, musing. "All the witchery of iron known to the nains might just suffice to mend them. But the Orfas King would not believe that. If these could be cured, he would expect, he would demand, he would require, that all the rotting iron in his realm be cured. And this cannot be done. I do not say it can never be done. But it cannot be done now. I do not know when. Perhaps never again in our lives— Dame—perhaps never in our lives—"

A moment's silence. "I shall leave them at the forge," she said. Again a moment's silence. Then she said and her beauty seemed no less than it had been that long ago when Uurtenokh-tenokh-guur had been a wandernain and she the lady of the Orfas Chief. He not yet king. She not yet queen. Sundry sayings floated in his mind. *One queen is every queen, every queen is all queens.* A beautiful woman, no doubt, and without question well versed in witchery, though he knew as little of queencraft as she of naincraft. She spoke again and said, "What have you to tell me of one who waits to return from across the all-circling sea?" He looked at her with pure unknowing and the certainty ebbed from her face. Then she said, "One who is not to be named, one who is the son of the half-brother—"

Understanding seemed to come not so much from his mind as from his broad and grizzled chest, whence a sigh of comprehension welled "Ahhh. That one, who contested with—Nay, Dame, I haven't seen that one for four handfuls of seasons. Eh, must be full four. Nor heard of that one in that time. Say you that he has passed the all-circling seas?"

She gazed at him, a line between her brows. "Say you not? I see you seem full ignorant of what I had thought every nain, as every man, has heard: that one fled to the barbar-

lands after fleeing court—when my Orfas gained the kingship—and has conspired to curse the iron so that, when he
returns with hordes of barbar-folk, the kingsmen shall be as
though unarmed. And say you that you know this not?"

He stretched forth both his long, long arms and held up
both his thick and calloused palms—straight up—and he
looked at her with pure unknowing.

~ ~ ~ ~ ~

LONG he sat there alone, musing on what she had said, striving to make sense of it. Long he sat there, reflecting on old
conflicts long forgotten—though clearly not forgotten by the
Orfas King. Long he sat there, yearning for the red fires and
the hot forges and the lust and joy of beating out the good
red iron. Old forge songs and sayings came to him and old
sayings not of the forge at all, such as *By three things only
can a king be made: by strength, by magic, and by fortune.*

Having set in the outercourt a watch of mandrakes who
would shriek beshrew if so much as unhidden shadow fell,
Merreddelfen, the principal witcherer, and the king and
queen sat in the Room of Secret Counsel.

Said the queen, "What news?"

Said the king, "What help?"

Said the sage, "Much news, little help."

In his mind he said, *Little news, no help.* But one did not
say such dire words, doom words, to the king. "Slayer of
SpearTeeth, the Painted Men report a spy in the forest. I have
no fear; the spy is dead."

Said the king, "Why dead? Why dead? From a dead spy
no news can be gotten."

Said the queen, "Why not dead? A dead spy betrays no
secrets."

Said the sage, "Great Dire Wolf, a dream has been
dreamed of All-Caller, the great fey horn. No doubt this por-
tends great good and who better to enjoy great good than
thee, Great Dire Wolf?"

Said the king, "Ah."

Said the queen, "Oh."

Said the sage, "Woe."

Said the king and queen, "*What?*"

Said the sage quite swiftly, "Woe to the enemies of the King of Thule, the Slayer of Bull Mammonts, the Great Dire Wolf."

Said the sage quite slowly, "Wearing my Cloak of Night, I crept to the mines; there I heard the nain-thralls chanting in the Old Language, singing in the Magic Tongue. Lord and Lady, they intoned a tale of Fireborn, a thing of witchery of which they said it will cut good iron. *Good iron!*—Lord and Lady! And if the nainfolk make words about good iron, is this not a sign that the nains know that iron will soon be as good as iron was before?"

Said the sage quite steadily, "Lady, you must use all your ways and wiles. Lady, you must prepare for many journey-ings. Lady, you must wear many masks."

Then they set their heads even closer together and they whispered and nodded and bit their lips. The mandrakes mut-tered. And the shadows danced.

~ ~ ~ ~ ~

THE breadth of the cavern was one nain wide and the height of the cavern was one nain high. Soldier guards, kingsmen, were obliged to stoop. More than once when the nain-thralls had been ordered to make the roof higher they expressed a gruff unwillingness to do so, saying that the roof would fall. So the guards were obliged to swing sideways the cudgels with which they struck the nain-thralls if the nains did not hack their stone-mattocks into the crumbly ironrock swiftly enough or if they lingered or stumbled while carrying the baskets of ore up the long incline and up the risky ladders set in shallow steps—up, up and up to the open sky inside the grim stockade.

Not long ago the notion of nain-thralls had only belonged to the past—a subject for winter tales or summer-night song-show, in the days of bronze—when no king reigned—the nain-thralls dug the brazen-ore * and forged the brazen-tools, how the greensickness came upon Thule and all bronze died and Chaos was king; how the nains discovered the secret witchery of iron and were free men at all times after, only paying the nainfee to the man king who in subduing the chiefs succeeded them as Power.

Thralldom was still the subject of song and story—or rather, again.

But who cared what dirges the nains sang as they toiled or what accounts they told as they lay on their beds of bracken in their imprisoned nights?

The swans fly overhead
And the nains see them.
The moles tunnel through the earth
And the nains see them.
Stockades do not wall the swans
And the nains see them.
Fetters do not bind the moles
And the nains see them.

The baskets of ore were emptied into hand barrows and the thralls carried the barrows to the forge.

Once the nains were free as swans
And the nains see them.
Once the nains were free as moles
And the nains see them.

The forge was a flat rock rising from deep under the ground. The fire burned upon a hearth of other flat rocks, raised to a platform of the same height as the forge. The lumps of ironstone (and the articles of sick iron) were placed in the fire and burned. Although the kingsmen walked to and fro in violation of the ancient compact which excluded them as it did all strangers, they learned nothing from their observations that did them any good. All ores looked alike to

---

* Although the presence of bronze as a crude earth is very rare, it is not unknown.

them; they did not know which ones to discard. All fired ironstones remained mysteries still to them; they knew not, though the nains did, which ones to discard as too brittle and which to pull out with greenwood toolsticks to be pounded upon the forge stone. Nor did they learn (or very much attempt to learn) the art of smiting with the stout stone hammer, turning and beating, beating and turning—all the while intoning in the Old Tongue:

> *Pound it, pound it, pound it well,*
> *Pound it well, well, well,*
> *Pound it well, pound it well,*
> *Pound it well, well, well . . .*

because it was said, *The sound of the voice is good for the iron . . .*

~ ~ ~ ~ ~

PERHAPS it was no longer as good as it once had been. Nothing seemed to be. Day after day the nains toiled to make new iron, hacks and spears and knifeheads and arrow points. And day after day the productions of—at first—the previous year were returned to them, rotten with rust, flaking and powdering, to be melted down and made new and whole again. The previous year— at first. Then the irons of the previous half-year. Then the previous season. Then last week, month—last fortnight.

One sweating nainsmith paused and pointed to a red-sick lancehead and his chest, thick and thicketed as some woodland hill, swelled as he spoke. "Not a seven-night since I beat this out—and now look how swift the iron-ill has afflicted it!" And he added in the witchery-tongue: "Thou art sick, thou art sick. Alas and woe to thee and us for thy very sickness."

And in his rumbling, echoing voice he began to chant and was joined by his thrall-fellow:

> *Woe for the iron that is sick,*
> *And the nains see it.*
> *Woe for the black stone whose red blood wastes.*
> *And the nains see it.*

He thrust the heap of rusted metal into the wood fire, deep, deep, till red coals and red metals met.

> *Woe for the king whose men take captive,*
> *And the nains see it.*
> *They take captive upon the paths,*
> *And the nains see it.*
> *They lead away in heavy ropes,*
> *And the nains see it.*
> *Captivity and toil lay waste the heart.*
> *And the nains see it.*
> *Captivity and toil lay waste the flesh,*
> *And the nains see it.*
> *The nain-thralls waste like iron,*
> *The king's evil is like rust,*
> *The queen's lust is wasteful, evil,*
> *Evil, evil, are these times,*
> *These days, consumed as though by wolves.*
> *When will the wolf confront the bear,*
> *And the nains see it?*
> *When will the stars throw down their spears?*
> *And the nains see it?*
> *Confusion take these smooth of skin*
> *And the nains see it?*
> *When will the wizards' mouths be fed,*
> *And the nains see it?*

The nainsmith seized a lump of iron and beat upon it with the stone hammer with great, resounding blows; and with each blow they all shouted a word:

> *When! Will! This! King-! -dom!*
> *Rot! And! Rust!*
> *And! The! Nains! See! It!*

IV

STRANGE SOUNDS HE heard as he lay between earth and sky, rising and sinking, turning over and over again. Strange calls upon strange horns, strange voices, sounds. Pains, swift and passing like flashes of lightning, shot through him, again and again, then less often. The Painted Men were pursuing him; he hid from them; he hid in hollows beneath the roots of trees, he hid in the forks of the branches of trees, perched upon the crests of rocks, slid into the spaces between them. Always, always, saw the Painted Men prance by, panting in rage and shame that he had seen their naked skin. Always, always he stayed quite still. And always, always, they passed him by. And always, always they paused, legs frozen in mid-stride.

And always they turned, saw him; he felt the blows; all vanished.

Years went by.

~ ~ ~ ~ ~

WHEN he became aware that he was returning to the everyday world he said in his mind that he would be very cunning and not reveal that he was no longer in the other world. He lay very still. Perhaps the Painted Men were uncertain if he were alive or dead and were lying in wait to see. He could not, through his parted eyelids, observe anyone or anything at all, save for the green network surrounding him and through which faint glints of sky were visible. But he had a faint yet firm feeling that if he were to roll his eyes just a bit to the right— He did not; he was too canny for that.

Besides, his right eye seemed swollen so much that—

And then a hand appeared, small as that of a large child, delicate as that of a young woman, yet not either: in the dim green light and through only one and a half eyes the hand seemed not entirely real, seemed almost translucent, had something about the bone structure, the nails—how many joints were there—nacreous as the inside of certain sea or river shells.

The hand placed something on his puffed eye, something cool and damp and soothing.

. . . and without awareness of intent to do so, he put up his hand and took the other by the wrist and sat up. Almost, he had not held the hand at all. Almost, it was as if his fingers were encircling something which had dimension without having substance—a delicate flower, as it might be, in the shape of a hand—and it slipped out from his grasp as simply as a sunbeam.

He had never seen a perry before.

Something slipped off his eye—he saw it was a dressing of bruised leaves and grasses, damp as though with the morning's dew: the perry's delicate and almost insubstantial hand took it and placed it on the swollen eye again and the perry's other hand took his hand, did not so much lift as guide it to hold the compress in place.

As the thin dew sparkling upon a cobweb, so did the perry's garments glint and sparkle; as the shy fawn stands in the gladey underbrush, not quite trembling and not quite looking at the intruder but poised for instant flight, so did the perry stand at the entrance to the leafy bower.

Arnten's body did not so much still pain him as it echoed faint reflections of remembered pain. Dim outlines of bruises he could see here and there upon his skin; he remembered enough lore of herbs and simples from his medicine uncle to know that even the most puissant leaves or roots or grasses had not by themselves done all this work of healing: but the witchery of the perries, either intent or inherent or both, had aided them. At first he had had a fleeting thought that he might be in the hands of The Woman of the Woods, of whom many tales were told. To be sure, he had never seen the Woman of the Woods, just as he had never seen a perry—but his uncle had told him enough of each so that now he knew. His uncle who was his mother's uncle. His mother whom he had lost.

Arnten, find your father.

His father whom he had never had. The bear he could not find. The man, the mocker (had said Long Roke) who had "gamed" his mother. The bogey for whom the boys of the village had held him slightly in awe and so much in scorn. Because of whom he had fled for very life. In which flight he had all but lately lost his life. And now lay here, back from the edge of death, in the company of a creature far more fey than any nain, who spoke no word and barely looked at him and barely smiled yet had felt that deep concern for him and even now trembled between visibility and invisibility, substance and shadow, staying and leaving.

This gentle presence touched the cords which bound his pent misery and long-contained sorrow and did that which heavy and brutal blows had not and could not have done, and he covered his face with his hands and broke into tears.

He wept long and without restraint and when he had stopped at last, he knew it would be long, if ever, before he wept again. His eyes were wet and his chest ached, but these were slight shadows which would pass. All his body aches had gone. Something had changed in him forever. He dried his eyes, including the one no longer swollen—and he was on his knees and rising when he realized that the perry was no longer there.

~ ~ ~ ~ ~

HE WAS aware of hunger and thirst, but more of thirst. He was aware of something else, a sound that had been sighing in his ears for as long as he had been in this shelter which somehow the perry had made for him. Sometimes the sound was as faint as a baby's breath; sometimes it grew almost as loud as the wind which carried it and sometimes louder, the rider overbearing the steed. Somewhere not so very far away was a river and now, in this moment of his great thirst (water perhaps needed to replenish that shed by his uncommon tears), great was the sound of its rushing.

The perry had stood upright, but Arnten found he was obliged to stoop, although certainly the grasses and the light,

light withes would have yielded easily to his head. And so, while at the curiously woven opening, stooping slightly and about to go out, he became aware of two things lying almost concealed by the fragrant grasses of the shelter's floor. One was the witchery-bundle to which both bark basket and knife had been tied by deft and curious perry-knots; the other re-appeared to him as though out of his dreamworld between the time the Painted Man had beaten him to the ground and the time of his reawakening.

He recalled it now. When he had felt (and doubtless had indicated) thirst, something had glowed and glittered in the air before him, touched his lips and he had drunk. He had in his semithoughts believed it a fragment of a rainbow convey-ing the cooling rainwater to his lips; or a gigantically dis-tended drop, suffused with multicolored lights, distilling into water on his lips and tongue. Now he saw it to be, less fan-tastically but not much less wondrously, a flask of some sub-stance unfamiliar to him. Light passed into it and through it and he voiced wordless surprise on observing that he could see *through* it! What he saw was subject to a gross distortion. The flask was iridescent as the fingernails of the perry or the interior of certain shells, shining with a multitude of colors which shifted and changed. And it weighed much less than a vessel of earthenware of the same bulk. He marveled, but did not stop for long to do so; he placed it in the basket along with the witchery-bundle (knife again by hip); he considered what its name might be. For present identification alone he deemed to call it perryware.

And then he stepped outside, ready to seek his stream.

The sound of the river was quite strong outside the small grass shelter, shelter so slight that seemingly a fawn could have crushed it by rolling over, now that the protecting pres-ence of the perry was withdrawn. He saw no traces of a fawn, but pausing a moment and wondering what, had cropped the small measure of meadow, greenery and flowery, he saw the pellet droppings of the wild rams and— his eyes now opened—here a shred and there a fluff of their wool. His uncle had at one time amassed a small heap of their hooves (begged, doubtless, from hunters) which lay a long while in a corner, oily and strong-smelling. Once a nain had come to trade new iron for old and the rams' hooves had vanished—but for what consideration and for what purpose he had never asked and never learned.

The wind brought the river sound stronger, nearer, to his ears; the wind brought a scent of flowers, too. He was on a downward slope and in a moment, following the land contours, he found himself wading through the blossoms—first they were under his feet, then around his ankles; then they touched the calves of his legs, his knee—and he brushed them away from his face. Glancing at his hands, he saw blood.

Astonished, he looked around. Each clump of flowers grew from a fleshy green pod. Pod? Paw? There had been a wild catton in the village once, though not for long. Taking amiss being prodded with a stick as it lay stretching with paws outthrust, out from those paws it thrust its claws and struck—once—twice—at its tormentor. Who in one moment more had crushed its skull with a rock. So, now: even as he half-halted his movements he saw a cluster of flowers dip down toward him, thrust out a sheaf of thorns and rake his chest with them. And then another. And then another. His arms, his legs, his back—he cried out, looked back, was struck again, flung his arms up before his eyes and staggered forward, raked with thorns and racked with pain. Then vinelets wrapped around his ankles . . . And then, for a long moment, nothing.

~ ~ ~ ~ ~

CAUTIOUSLY he opened his eyes. At once his ears seemed to open, too. There was a deep, intent humming in the air. He saw the thorn-paws of the thickets sway and waver. He saw them droop. He saw a swarm of bees spread out, circle; saw, one by one, the thorns draw back into their pods; saw the flowers open wider. Saw each bee select its first flower, mount and enter, heard the bumbledrone alter in pitch and quicken. Saw each plant stretch itself taut, then begin a slow undulant motion.

Saw himself utterly forgotten and ignored.

Once again had the wary feeling of being watched.

Saw nothing.

Made his way unvexed to the water, kneeled and drank.

Here the water rushed noisily over the rocks, there it eddied and circled silently into pools, out farther it glided with a joyful clamor along its main channel; then paused and murmured thoughtfully among the reeds. Everywhere it sparkled—in his cupped hands as he lifted it to his mouth, as it fell in droplets from his face, spun around sunken logs, made the reeds rustle. Something was trying to tell him— what? The reeds nodded.

Reeds.

With a movement so quick and unstudied that he sank one foot into water, he stood up, spun around and unslung his witchery-bundle—or, more exactly, the witchery-bundle supposedly left by his father—and spread out its contents in the sunshine. Fingers trembling, he unsheathed the knife and cut a fresh reed and laid it down beside the one in the bundle. Except that one was dry and one was fresh, they were identical.

Surely it was a sign.

The medicine objects restored to their coverings, he considered long what he should do. It seemed somehow natural that he should continue along the river; there, where he had found the first sign, might he not find at least a second?

At first he splattered along on the sand flats and gravel beds, the mudbanks and shallows of the shore. The river looked so wild, so wide, full of mystery (and, perhaps, menace). Here presently the salmon would come surging upstream, that was certain, but not now. What else might lie beneath those sounding waters was uncertain indeed. Sometimes the forest came right down to the brim and barm as though the trees would dip and drink. Sometimes he walked beneath towering banks and bluffs. After a while he saw the river divide and flow around an island, the main channel to the far side, the hither side forming a quiet pool, the shore of which was a sandy beach. On impulse he stopped, scooped out a hollow, placed into it his bundle and his basket with the perry thing, covered all with his leathern kilt, heaped sand over it. Then he turned and walked into the water.

~ ~ ~ ~ ~

THE shallows had been sunwarmed, but now the deeper and cooler waters began to lap against his legs, higher and higher, and he saw and felt the flesh about each hair creep into a tiny mound. He saw that hair was now growing thicker about his man-parts. Abruptly, with a slight gasp, he slipped deliberately beneath the surface and for a moment squatted on the bottom like a frog. His breath heaved against his chest. He opened his eyes. All was strange in this new world. Then something was suddenly familiar; he opened his mouth and only the sudden burst of bubbles reminded him that water and not air was his surrounding. He surfaced, took another breath, slid down once more. In the curious light he exchanged quick glances with a small fish, then bent his eyes to the river bottom. Green light wavered in the green water and rippled over the green stones.

Reed in his medicine bag, reed beside the water.

Greenstone in his medicine-bag, greenstones beneath the water.

It was the sought-for second sign.

The boy-frog squatted on the sand, sand clinging to him here and there, and looked at the other two small things in his budget of wonders: the beechnut and the bear claw. Certainly the last was the Sign of the Bear himself, and by now it was plain that what the bear was saying was, *Seek these others if you would seek me. Find these others and you will find me.* In the way a scout leaves signs along a trail so that those who follow may see and know what his message is, so the Bear had left these signs—not indeed in any sequence set apart by space—so that one who followed after might follow farther yet.

All clear, that. But what was the meaning of the beechnut? Beechnuts were good to eat, though perhaps not very good. The black swine of the woods were said to be fond of them. It wasn't clear what connection the wild swine had with the bear. Perhaps none. He began to feel confused and set his thoughts to tracing their way as though through a forest path: Bear—black swine—beechnut—well enough, by working backward he had come at least to some certain thing—beechnut—forest—trees—

Beechnuts, whatever else they indicated, certainly indicated a beech tree.

Not bothering to brush the sand from his bare legs and bottom, not from the leather kilt he swiftly and absently donned, he slung on his gear once more and set off along the river. But this time he walked along the dry land and looked, not down, but up. And so, by and by, by its silver-gray bark and its pale green leaves, but most of all its height, he saw the trees he sought. Some long past storm or earthshake, or perhaps a hidden subsidence of the ground beneath its roots, had inclined it at a slight angle, for it was near enough the river for the stream in spate to have undercut and then covered up its excavating—or, perhaps the blow of a thunderstone had bent it; above the lowest branch, many times his own length high over his head a great scar was burned into the massive trunk.

Once again he had the feeling of being watched; the feeling ebbed again.

And there was certainly no sight nor sign of a bear.

~ ~ ~ ~ ~

His disappointment was great. It would have been easy to stumble or falter, only that day's morning had he gotten up from a daze of illness which had lasted— he realized he did not know for how long—and he had barely paused for rest. He had drunk once. He had not eaten. Weakness rose inside him. What had he expected? To find his father and, in finding him, an end to all mystery and aloneness forever? Had he expected to find a father sitting at the bottom of the huge beech tree, ready to welcome him with warm embrace? Here he was, Arnten, and he was as alone, as hungry, as unknowing as he had ever been.

What then was he to do? Slump behind the shelter of a bush and sleep and die? Weakness vanished. The very force of its sensation became a strength that blazed up within him and made itself felt without. He felt his skin tingle with something close to rage against this curious father who had cost his mother's life, had never come near to see what he had begotten, had left his cryptic messages with the nains alone. A father who might be dead, long dead.

Had he been pursuing a ghost? Had he himself perhaps died already under the blows of the Painted Man and was now himself but a ghost? Did ghosts hunger? He allowed himself a cry of anger and bafflement. Then, fiercely, he filled his bark basket with such nuts and berries and leaves and shoots of greenfood as were close to hand. At a small trickle on its way to join the stream, he filled the perryware flask, stoppered its neck with a plug of fern. He arranged everything to hang behind him. Then, angry and hot-eyed, defiant and determined, he set his toes and fingers in the cracks and ridges of the beech tree's bark and began to climb. For the first time he allowed himself to speak his thoughts aloud.

"I will go up!" he said, through his set teeth. "I-will-go-up!" He inched up. And up. "And I *will* find out!" The bundle and basket dangled, swung out, bumped back, grew heavier. "And until I find out—" he panted, dug in once more, advanced, advanced—"I will not come down—"

He swung one leg over the lowermost branch, hoisted himself up, pressed his head to the rough bosom of the tree and hung on for very life against the wave of vertigo which threatened to plummet him to the ground. Slowly it passed and slowly he opened his eyes. The lazy wind swung into his face, laden with scents of the rich earth, of flowers and other growing things. He looked over leagues of land and the swelling and falling away of hills, the glittering serpentine length of the river, forest forever a great green roof. And far, far off, so distant that he could not be sure, he thought he saw thread-thin smoke. It might have been his village. He thrust forward his chin so suddenly that he felt a creak in his neck and, with all his force and might, spat in its direction. And then he allowed himself to realize that the lightning-burn upon the tree, just above the branch, was actually a tree-cave, a hollow.

It was, he considered (with a shiver), too small to harbor either tiger or leopard; it even lacked the reek of a bird's nest. Serpents would not go so high. Slowly, cautiously, he passed himself into it. Part of the bark still lay in place like a shell. And, patiently awaiting his discovery, wedged with splits of wood, protected from the worst assaults of the weather, was another hide-bound bag. Inside this was a box of carved wood. And in the box, padded with red-dyed fleece, was something that lay almost outside all his experience. Long he crouched in the dim light, half-afraid to touch it; then his fingers played over the intricate carvings. There was mammont-ivory and horn of wild ram, horn of elk; there was bear claw, there was—there were many things. Parts of it moved around, circle-wise, when he turned them. Parts moved up and down from holes, like little levers, when he touched them. Shapes of beasts and birds were carved into it. No man—nor nain—nor perry—had devised it. It was wizards' work, and wizardry of witchery alone. It was a witchhorn, so huge and adorned and complex it could only be the witchhorn. Could only be All-caller, the great, fey horn.

V

SEE THEN, IN the late rays of the afternoon sun, while the great red circle still throws heat before descending for its slow journey through the Cavern Beneath The Earth whence it will rise again next morning, a small, a very small Something sticking out its head from the bole of the huge beech tree. After the head, an arm, at the end of the arm a hand and in the hand—what? It is needful to come closer. A shaggy boy, not quite a new young man, excitement and triumph and also fear upon its mold-smutched face. Carefully he holds the great horn in both his dirty hands. Carefully he examines it yet again, turning its turnable parts.

Ah. Ahah. So. Here is the bear claw, as like to the bear claw in his witchery-bundle to make one think they had come from the same bear-beast. As, perhaps they had.

The boy's full lips protrude, compressed in thought. So— here is the bear carved in ivory upon the horn band. Surely it was meant to come in apposition to the bear claw. He takes a deep breath, fills his dusty cheeks, lifts the horn to his lips. His eyes roll, his nostrils distend.

And below upon the mossy ground, while the echoes of the great cry, part growl, part roar, still send the birds whirling about and the leaves quivering, something comes into the open glade around the beech tree. Something comes as though the thicket were mere fern grass. Something comes crashing, comes trampling, comes on all fours, comes walking upright. Stands, stopping. Peering this way and that. Paws and head swaying. Issues a cry, part roar, part growl. Part challenge, part question. Puzzled. Vexed. Brute. Bewildered.

Bear.
Bear.
Bear.

A moment passes, or does not pass; endures without end. Then the bear coughs, grunts, sighs, brushes at one ear. Gurgles deep within its shaggy chest. Ambles and shambles down to the river. Stands there without motion. Then makes

gestures which no bear has ever before been seen to make—
or so it seems to the watcher up high. Who has ever seen a
bear take off its skin before? Who has ever seen a man inside
a bear before? Who has ever seen a man stride into the water
and leave an empty bearskin lying on the bank behind, gap-
ing empty, eyeholes looking up, sightless, at the sky?

Has anyone—?

—before?

~ ~ ~ ~ ~

ARNTEN plucked up his talisman and, though it was the fa-
miliar-most of any object he had with him, he studied it as
though he had never seen it before. Almost, for that matter,
he had never seen a bear before. Perhaps he had seen live
bears one or two times—dead ones, before they had been all
skinned and dismembered for food and hide, several times.
The carving did not seem to have changed. The bear was still
certainly a bear—except that it still certainly had man's feet.
He could not recall that he had ever observed the feet of living bears, these must have been concealed in grass or underbrush, or perhaps he had just not been looking; likelier he
had had his eyes (as he crouched fearfully out of sight) on
the paws of the forelimbs, on the fearsome jaws. Perhaps *all*
bears had man's feet. But then a clear picture came to him of
the four paws of one dead bear, cut off for the pot—and all
were *paws*, none truly feet. And yet, might it not be that
bears, alive, had feet like men, and that these changed at
death? As for the bear below? Truly, he had not noticed. He
did not know.

Well, regardless, he knew what he had to do now.

He watched the man (formerly bear) swimming strongly
in the water, bobbing under, emerging with hair all sleek,
shaking his head, then resuming his swim, finally passing out
of sight around a bend in the river. He would certainly be
back. But Arnten was certain that he would not be back at
once. Unencumbered by any burdens, all of which he left in
the hollow, he climbed carefully down; he ran, eyes racing

between three places—the ground, lest he stumble—the water, lest the man, returning, see him soon—the bearskin, lest—lest what? Lest, perhaps, and most horrifying by far, the empty skin somehow take on life and move, either toward or away from him. For a second it did indeed seem upon the point of doing so and he gasped in fright. But it was only the wind raising a worn corner.

He seized the skin and ran, flinging it across his shoulder and feeling it on his back, bounding and bouncing. He could see it, feel it, thankfully he could not hear it, he had no desire or reason to taste it. He could smell it, though, and its reek was very strong, partly bear, partly man. All these things he perceived without being aware of concentrating on them. He concentrated first on getting out of sight of the water. And then he paused to think of what he should do next.

And, with a start, realized that he had already done something. Perhaps he should not have, perhaps he should return and undo it. But he knew he would not. That which he had so greatly desired, the one whom he had so straightly sought, the source of his being and his childhood's woe, man or bear or manbear or bearman, the witchery creature which had been his weakness and must now be his strength . . .

"I am afraid," he whispered.

True, That One In The Water clearly had desired to see him, had left a trail for him to follow perhaps not as clearly as if it had been blazed, as if it had consisted of traditional and familiar hunters' marks or patterns (but blazing and patterning were not intended to be other than open for all who could to read). And yet—and yet, why had he intended that his son should some day follow? How sure he had felt the son would follow, would meet the nains, would understand the messages bound up in the witchery-bundle: but this was for the moment beside the point and the point was the bearman / manbear was power, and power, as much as it was to be desired, so much was it to be feared.

Presently something showed itself in the river, moving against the current. Arms flashing in the declining sunlight. A figure came padding out of the water on a sandbar, moving as a bear does on all fours, but was not a bear; moved to the other end of the sandbar, where, motionless, it seemed to be staring into the water. A forelimb moved so fast that the motion could hardly be followed. Something flew out of the water, sparkled, fell. Twice more was the scene repeated before, now walking upright, a fish in each hand and one in the mouth, the figure walked through the water to the shore and shambled up the bank. Another, smaller figure, watching, trembled. The tall one was thickly built, with hair (now slicked down flat with water) so thick that almost the skin could be termed a pelt. It seemed that all the brightness of the sky of Thule, which had only an hour ago been evenly divided, was now moved and crowded to one side and that side so much brighter; while a blue dimness gathered on the other side. The birds began to fall silent. The air grew cool. Leisurely, the tall figure ambled up the slope and onto the bluff. The fish fell from its hands and mouth and it dropped backward so that it came to rest sitting down, legs straight out and arms crooked upright from the elbows. It gave a great roar of disbelief and rage. Then it rose and stabbed at the mossy ground and took up something in its hands.

The talisman, the wooden carving . . .

Then the head rose and scanned the bluff, the brush, the crowded arbor of the forest. Abrupt growls came from the thick chest formed themselves into rage words.

"Where are you?

"Why have you done this?

"Where is my skin?"

A voice came from somewhere up above, from the thickening darkness. "I will not answer your questions till you have answered mine."

"Ask, then—"

And the other voice, a moment silent, wavering a bit, but not halting, said, "Who are you? Who am I? What is next?"

~ ~ ~ ~ ~

APPROPRIATELY the backlog of the fire had come from the great beech tree. "Long since I have made fire, or eaten food cooked on it, or food with salt on it," said Arntat. His hands, however, seemed to have lost no skill. The fish had been deftly gutted, gilled and grilled. Salt, in a screw of barkrag, was still in Arnten's basket. "Salmon will be better," Arntat said, smacking his mouth at the thought. "But these are well enough." Sparks leaped, embers blackened, glowed again. Abruptly he swiveled and faced the boy. "You be thinking, 'Is it to hear talk of fish and fire that I've come this long way, waiting?' Eh? I see it by your face, 'tis so. Arnten. I have waited longer than you. Be patient."

And the boy was silent.

~ ~ ~ ~ ~

AND his fullfather said, "The bear is in the blood and the bear may take you as the bear took me. At any time whilest life blood be in you the bear may take you, for the bear is in the blood. If it takes you not, and it may not take you, if it takes you not then 'twill take your son and if not you and not him then 'twill take your son's or daughter's son for sure. Let this be no burden. Fear it not. I've dabbled and dallied with a queen of love, and though 'twas joyous passion, yet 'twas nought compared to shambling 'mongst the new berries or finding honey in a tree or scooping forth first salmon, when I was gone a-bearing," his fullfather said.

And he said, "Bear's weird be better than man's weird and better than nain's weird. As a man I've been a chieftain high with lands and wealth—you may let your ears drop, 'tis nought to you *where* and nought to you *what's-my-name-then*. You were not made upon empty bear hide in lawful bedchamber, ah no, you were made when the bear was in the bearskin. My heritage to you is other than to my othergotten sons. Heed and hear me now, Arnten. By my witch-bundle and by my shadow, sons you make outside the bearskin be outside the bear-blood. But sons you make when you be a-bearing and be inside the bearskin, the blood of the bear be in them. And if the blood of the bear be in them, then not running water nor icy pools nor firehot springs can wash it out."

And the bear was silent.

~ ~ ~ ~ ~

BEECHWOOD makes hard embers and hard embers make long fires. Long fires make long tales. Long they sat there in the scented night and Arntat talked and Arnten listened and learned. He learned that the shift and shape was truly not confined to man to bear, that other creatures indeed could pair, could couple, could double and shift.

> *Bee and salmon, wolf and bear,*
> *Tiger, lion, mole and hare . . .*

He learned of the slow growth of metals beneath the earth's skin and the formation of amber beneath the sea, how amber was one of the things of the perries, whereas metal was a thing of the nains. Once there was a metal called bronze but at length it grew green and sick and presently it died. Now there was iron.

"The sickness of iron is red," said Arnten, "and iron is dying." Red glints in the ashes. Reflections in the eyes of the watchers.

"Aye, eh." muttered Arntat. "The sickness of iron is red." He swung up his head and his hand gripped his son's. "What say thee, bear's boy? '*Iron is dying?*' What?"

That he, knowing so much, should not know this, for several heartbeats kept Arnten silent and astonished. Then he saw pictures in his mind: one: one: then he saw things moving, heard the nain tell of years since "Bear" was by them seen. Arnten said, "You have been long inside the bearskin, then, and that long you've not seen iron?"

Still the hand gripping his did not move. "*Iron is dying?* True, true, many springtimes I have caught and killed the great salmon and many summertimes I have climbed for honey in the honeytrees and in the rocky clefts. Many falltimes have I eaten the last of the frost-touched fruits and the sweet flesh of nuts. And many wintertimes have I felt the bearsleep come upon me and felt the numbness grow inside my head and sunk into the lair till the snows grow thinner. Aye. Eh. I can count the time only by counting your time. You are barely a man. And the last iron I had seen, the last iron I had thought of, I wrapped well the iron knifelet in my witchery-bundle and hid it well for thee. May it be sick?"

Arnten did not mind the grip upon his hand. He crouched against the crouching body of his fullfather. He rested on that puissant flesh which had made his own and which was now his present as well as his past. Defying mankind and beastkind and time and the night, he let himself recline against the great rough beast which was his father and he let his hand recline in that great rough paw. Quietly, almost drowsily he said, "That witchery-knife alone is not sick. But all other iron is sick." And he muttered, "The nains," and he muttered of the nains. And he sighed, "The king—" and he sighed words of the king. And almost he fell asleep, comforted by the rough, warm body and its rough and powerful smell. Then the body moved, releasing his hand, and a sound which was almost a cry and almost a groan rumbled and broke loose from that strong fatherbody by the embers.

"*Iron*!

"*The nains*!

"*The king*!"

Almost he flew awake. He slid down so that he might stand up. The day had been long and there was still much to talk about. The day had begun with the mammont hunt and he had run far and he had been hurt and nains and perries and Painted Men pursued him and he ran along the river and now the long long day was over and he had nevermore again to run to bolt to flee and *Iron*! *Sick iron*! *The wizards*! and *The king*! sounded their names in the darkness. And the embers slid down because they were tired and the embers slipped beneath the ashes and the embers slept.

In the morning the embers were awake again and spitting and flaring at the meat that turned, spitted and smoking. Arntat was still crouched by the fire as though he had never left it and as though the meat had come at his bidding and obediently slipped out of its skin and onto the spit. Arntat yawned hugely and glanced at Arnten and it seemed as though his teeth were still the tushes and the fangs of Bear, his eyes still Bear's eyes so small and cunning and sharp, his blunt face still Bear's muzzle and his hairy hands with long thick nails— The yawn closed with a snap.

The man said, "There was the lone one of you?"

"The—"

"Sometimes a she kindles with twain. Or more. My get, by your dam—"

"Only me, as I ever heard. I never knew her. Uncle said she drowned. Was mad."

Arntat grunted. "It was time for it to be done and I was there and she was there and 'twas done, so. If not she, another. If not me, another. If not she and me, then not thee." He took the spit from its forks and rested the savory roast, dribbling, on the grass. "So. The lone one of you. Called me from my bearguise." He seized his son by his downy shoulders. "Hid from me my bearskin." Son resisted, wordlessly, was pressed down nontheless. "Carried off with him my token. Found the nain. Found me. Called me from my bearguise. Stole away my bearskin. The lone one of you." Arnten was on his back, flat. "Am I to regret 'twasn' twins? Or be one of such enough?" The single hand quivered the boy belly as one would a pup's. Then moved, one hand, two hands, tore the roasted meat apart, slapped on part still sizzling on the place the hand had been—boy leapt up, yelping—bared his teeth and began to eat.

Boy teeth shining sharp in quick-closed mouth. Boy hand rubbing belly. Boy snout smelling savory food. Boy cub by bear man, tearing meat from bone.

Still eating when father got up and strode off, he followed at quick pace, still holding his own unfinished portion. "Arn!" he said. "Arntat! Bearfather!"

Bearfather growled over his shoulder.

"The hide! The horn! The witchery-bundle! Shall I fetch?"

Arntat growled, "The hide? Leave it be. I'll go no more abearing for now. The horn? Leave it be. Rather than call wrong, call none for now. The witcher-bundle? As you want." And he melted into the shadows of the all-circling forest. Arnten followed, thinking and eating as he went. Claw and reed and stone and nut, he had read their message and read them rightly; he could part with them for now. The hide with its medicine signs he needed not now. For a moment he begrudged the knife, the good knife of good iron. He took a longing look at the slightly slant and towering beech tree, casting a long shadow in the morning sun as it had cast in the evening. They were all safe up there in the hollow of the hideyhole. And there, safely, let them bide, then.

Still eating, he slipped after his father into the dappled surface of the forest.

~ ~ ~ ~ ~

ARNTAT did not precisely linger, he did not exactly dally, neither did he rush ahead with great speed, nor slink through the woods. Some sort of game was being played. For neither did Arnten go so fast as he might. It was the game, then, that each should generally hold the other in sight, but only generally. And sometimes the bigger one would suddenly hide himself and as suddenly reveal himself when the smaller paused to look around, then proceed as though he had not been hidden at all. Before long they had developed many aspects to this game and little tricks and presently they were again and again filled with silent laughter at each other. Through many a clearing and burn and along the paths they played their game, sometimes 'Tat leaping along a fallen tree as lightly as a squirrel, at least once 'Ten dropping several leaves before being realized and looked up at.

It lasted most of the morning and might have lasted much longer, but then Arnten, running noiselessly around a great lichen-studded boulder, ran full tilt into flesh which only in that first second he thought was his father's. A swift blow and an angry word undeceived him before his eyes did—he who had for all morning dropped even the memory of blows and angry words—and, as he tried to scramble to his feet, tried to turn his head to see who it was, tried (all these at once) to run away any which way, someone grabbed his arm and twisted it. Only then did he cry out.

The man's face had the look of one who kicks a dog not to be rid of it but for the pleasure of kicking it. Then the face changed and the arm released him, raised its spear; the mouth that cursed him gave a sick croak as something snapped which was not the spear. Arntat was there. Arntat was holding, embracing, Arntat was crushing. Ugly sounds of witless fright, then, from this other's mouth. Blood gushing from that mouth. And then other men, many other men, spears and clubs and then ropes, Arntat down on one knee. Arntat releasing limp and bleeding body, Arntat clawing out for a grip upon another. Arnten biting, beating. Arntat down. Arntat growling, roaring. Men cursing as much in fright as wrath. Arntat down. Arntat suddenly silent, save for his breathing in the sudden silence. Arntat bound. Arnten, too.

And after some moments of gasping, recovering breath, slowing hearts, hissing of pain, someone said as though to a question none had heard, "I don't know—I don't know— Eh? Ah? Nains? *No!* Nor bears—"

Another voice. "We be the king's men. Let the king say *what*." And others, others. "Aye! Ah! Let the king say what!"

VI

THE RED-SICKNESS of all iron flamed into a plague. At first whispered, it was now said openly that the king himself had caught the evil and the ill. Indeed, it seemed to be so. Red blotches were seen about his face and hands and all his face and limbs and frame looked wasted and hollowed. His voice cracked and croaked. His hands shook. In the mornings he groaned and staggered. In the late afternoons his eyes would roll up and his eyelids roll down and he folded his legs and lay where he happened to be, servants hastily bringing furs and fleeces and lifting him and settling him again. For the length of time it took for the shadow of the sun-staff to move over two stones the king at such times lay as one dead. And in the late night hours he tended to enrage easily, to shout and strike out and to cast things.

But in the early and middle afternoon and in the early and middle night times he was as well as ever in those days he was well. As to the first of these periods, it was assumed he was passing well, for his voice could be heard talking— talking, not groaning, not yelling—and as for the second of these periods, it was then that he held such gatherings as he held and saw such outsiders as he saw. In the red light of the hearth all men may look reddened and the dancing shadows may make all men look gaunted.

But not all men hide themselves in daylight.

Day by day the couriers trouped in. Night by night the king himself would see them and let himself be seen by them and from them receive the tidings which he had, of course, already received; for did he not sit upon his stool or lie upon his pallet behind the reed curtain while the courier made report upon the other side? Tirlagusak, grown stout and gray in his service as a first captain of the king's men, generally stood forth as the couriers came in, each with the strip of white bark cloth bound about his head, which even toddle-babes knew signified *I am the king's mouth and I am the kings eyes and I am the king's ears. Delay me not—and if I need aid, aid me.*

"Thirty-deer Hill," the courier might say. Or: "Whalefish Point."

Tirlag-usak puts out his hand. "Tally," he says. "Why so slow?"

The courier hands over the cut and carved piece of wood. He pants to show how hard he has run. Of late there had been increasingly less sham in this. Tirlag-usak, of course, knows whence every one of the couriers has come but he sees if the tallystick fits the proper one from his own box.

"Report sightings," he directs. "Swiftly."

"Good omens from the flocks of birds," says the courier. It would not do to report *No sighting*.

"Eat. Wash. Rest. Return after evening meal."

The courier retires, sweating but relieved. His tongue may be the king's tongue but that need not prevent it's being cut.

Behind the reed curtain the king's lips writhe, the king's hands move convulsively. The king's face grows redder yet. The redsickness increases fast upon him. And the red-sickness increases fast upon the iron. The courier has gone. Tirlag-usak remains standing. From behind the reed curtain comes an anguished whisper.

"Iron? *Iron?*"

"The ears of the king hear all things," says the grizzled first captain. After just a breath, he says, "The king already has heard that it is not better. It is not even as it was." After three breaths should come the groan or hiss which has come to mean *Go!* but Tirlag-usak today, after only two breaths, repeats, "The ears of the king hear all things." And says further, "The king has already heard that ten of his men who went north in a search for nains have this day returned with captives."

"*Uhh?*"

"One great and one small, as the king already has heard. The eyes of the king have already seen them and it may be that the king's eyes have already recognized one of them as the king's kin to whom the king's mouth will speak more words."

Tirlag-usak had spoken somewhat more rapidly than usual. Now he waits for the space of many breaths and he hears
each of these breaths from behind the reed curtain. But no
question now comes from behind the reed curtain and what
now comes thence at last is a cry of such agony and terror
and rage that almost the hand of Tirlag-usak touches the woven reed barrier—almost he stoops to lift it. But he hears
other feet, other voices, babble and whisper and shuffle and
sigh. Then nothing. Then, only then, he departs.

Later, in the enclosure where they were penned, Arnten
suddenly looked up. Arntat, his father, did not pause in his
shambling and shuffling, shuffling and shambling, back and
forth and back and forth, head weaving like a snake's head
from side to side. It seemed he did not share his son's
thought, a sudden one which projected into the boy's mind a
picture of the mandrakes dancing to the sound of the small
drum in his old uncle's medicine hut. The recollection was
so clear that the boy sat and watched it inside his head for
some time.

~ ~ ~ ~ ~

MERED-DELFIN beat the small drum and his mandrakes,
which were the mandrakes of the king and queen, danced
their witchery-dance and Mered-delfin watched them from
the corner of his eyes and the king and queen watched them
full front. Every feeling moved across the king's face, none
at all disturbed the face of the queen. The mandrakes moved
and the mandrakes moved and they mimed and mimed and
they danced. At first, coming forth from their carved wood
chest, the mandrakes' motion kept time to the tune of the
witchery-drumlet. But after a while and after Mered-delfin
had sung to them and hummed to them and chanted to them,
whistled and drummed to them, then the pattern of their
moving changed. They led and Mered-delfin followed, his
fingers and his palms straining to keep up with them, to
maintain the proper tune and rhythm upon the drumhead

made from the skin entire of a dwarf deer slain without bruise or blood.

At length, when they had begun to repeat themselves and no chantings or whistlings could prevail upon them to enact any new pattern, Mered-delfin drummed them back and dancing they went, throwing up their root-thin arms they danced backward upon their root-thin legs, and climbed back into their box at last and closed its lid upon them.

Thus the dancing mandrakes. As for the watching mandrakes, they remained in the outer court and would shriek, beshrew, if so much as an unbidden shadow fell. And there they muttered and watched.

The chief witcherer licked his mouth and wiped his arm across his sweat-slick face and quickly rolled his eyes. The other two were not looking at him. Swiftly he set his countenance into its accepted lines. He softly clicked his fingernail against the side of the drum. They looked up toward him.

"It is as we have seen, it is as I have said, they have enacted the lineaments of the dream and mimed for us the finding and the sounding of All-Caller, the Great Fey Horn—"

The king grimaced and showed his sharp teeth. As he leaned forward on his hands and arms he seemed to crouch on all fours. "And where, then," he asked, "is the great good which you said this dream portended for me?"

Mered-delfin parted his thin beard from lips and mouth and dared to grin. The very daring of the deed made the king draw back, somewhat relax the tenseness of his pose. Witch-Mered thrust out his hand and arm and described a quarter-circle in the air and let the hand extend two lingers in a point. "Can it be that the sounding of All-Caller has lured from across the all-circling sea an enemy who is not to be named? And with him a son begat in treacherous exile? Lured them thence and it must be alone?"

His master's grimace grew into a snarl. His eyes blazed red. He seemed like a creature of the forest about to hurl itself from its den. He gave off the rank and bitter smell of denizen and den. "I shall kill them!" His voice rose into a howl. "I shall have them killed! They shall be killed for me and before me!" His tongue lolled out of his mouth. "Limbs broken—" the howl prolonged itself—"impaled—"

"Slayer of Bull Mammonts—"

"—*flayed*—"

"Great Dire Wolf—"

"—*disemboweled*—"

The last word hung upon the air. The Orfas panted. His sides heaved. He flung up his head and again he howled. In this howl there were no words, but it rang with a lust for vengeance long delayed. In his narrow pen Arntat heard it and stopped in his mindless pacing and hearkened to it and his arms moved slightly and he stood still. The nain-thralls heard it in their tunnels and turned their massy heads on their short necks. Servants heard it and shivered and tremored. King's men felt flesh pucker and hair rise and let their eyes roll to each other, and almost they clean forgot the tales of the ill-struck king, cloistered and shabby and sick and old.

"The Orfas," they whispered to one another.

"The wolf! The wolf!"

"King Orfas! Great Wolf! King Wolf!"

"—*King Wolf*—"

~ ~ ~ ~ ~

LONG the wolf-king lay upon his side, panting, wet with sweat. Then he jerked his head and in two silent bounds Mered-warlock was crouching at his head. Said the king, "Not kill him?"

Said the witcherer, "Not yet."

Said the wolf-king, "When, then?"

Said the sage, "When the curse is canceled. When iron is well."

The king said no word. His eyes rolled up and his lids rolled down. He nodded. He touched his sage's hand. His queen kneeled beside him and he touched her face. The words last spoken hung upon the air.

And the words unspoken, too.

~ ~ ~ ~ ~

ARNTEN and his father were allowed to toil together; one of
the guards had said with a guffaw that the two of them were
barely equal to one nain. Iron was the nains' heritage and
though they had been used to it in all its workings at their
own speed and though timed toil was inhospitable to them,
still the nature of mining was not strange. But it was all
strange, strange and fell, to Arntat and his son. Only the un-
swerving friendship of the nains and the fact of his and his
son's being still together at all relieved the toil. And worse
by far than the toil was the circumstance of bondage, of con-
finement, of life now being limited to a set series of motions
within severely limited space. All thralldoms are one same
thralldom. The unremitting labor of the toil, the unremitting
oppression of the guards, the ill food, cramped space, un-
cleanliness, lack of hope, dull hatred, scanted sleep, infinite
heaviness of spirit—are not these the features of all thralldoms?

"It is harder, Bear, for thee than we," the nains said. "The
tunnel fits we as the hoodskin fits the pizzle."

"Then I stoop," he said. Stooped, grunted. "I have stooped
before." But his eyes were sunken. And his forehead bruised
and scabrous, for he did not always think to stoop, nor they
to warn him.

And the nains said, "It is harder, Bear, for thee than we.
We be used to the smell of iron dust and fire and have forgot
the smell of grass and waterflows."

"Then I shall grow used to this and shall forget that other,
too," he said. But he did not grow used to it, he often was
coughing, and there was that in his eyes and on his face
which seemed to show that he was not forgetting. And one
night when the begrudged fire burned low and the older
nains had begun to creep into their sleepy-holes and kick the
crushed bracken-fern into a brief semblance of softness—at
last that night his voice burst loud with, "But I cannot forget!
No! No! I cannot forget!"

The older nains crept out from their sleepy-holes, greasy-sided, fetid, close. They laid their hands on his, and on his knees and arms and legs, their huge and calloused hands. And a few did so to Arnten, who had crept close to his father; and the heavy nain-hands were light and gentle. "Since thee cannot forget, Bear, cease to try," they said. "And speak it out to we." And the Bear spoke.

Not—at first—of the free life of sun and stars, grass and waterflows, salmon hunts and honey thefts, of timeless days and world without walls. These all, it seemed, though well remembered in general, had become as it were a design bordered in dyed grasses around a basket rim—turn it, turn it, now faster, now slower, and see the same sequences following forever; man's mind no longer holding in differentiating recollection any one sequence from any other like it—so it seemed, when by and by his talk took up those days.

~ ~ ~ ~ ~

But he began with other days, when he was a man's child among other mens' children, he one and Orfas another and Orfas a little older. Not much difference in age and little if any in status, even after both presently realized that Orfas was in a way an uncle—that Orfas' father was the other's grandfather, the other's father Orfas' half-brother. Both playing and tumbling and chasing dogs in one familiar yard onto which opened (so it seemed) the doors of many houses, yet all of them family houses. In those days they were but two among many and each father had several sons and neither more of a rival to each other than either was to any others. All the sons and cousins and uncles of that age had cast their reed practice spears and away like the wild swans fly away, yet never do the absent years return as do the absent swans.

Boys had grown to men, passed through ordeal and initiation, learned which was their witcherybeast, dreamed medicine dreams, had found women and knew the milk of life to be within them. The hunt had ceased to be play and often man had fought with man, not for proving or for pleasure but for very life; and some had taken life and some had lost it. Some of all that company of boykin had died young beneath the feet or claws or within the jaws of wild beasts or had been dragged down beneath the waves by waterkelpies or by fierce hippotames. Others had made themselves house-holders and gotten children while still barely bearded. Some had sought a name and fame by captaining pursuits of whale-fish or werewhales, tree-tigers, or had gone north into the snows to hunt the wild leopard. One had been allured by the bewitchments of the Painted Men (whose skin must not be-seen).

"There was a certain great tree whose wide-spreading branches we all climbed as boys. It became our gathering place and remained so even when we were men and gathered there more seldom. But whenever we so returned, there we went and there we looked to meet with our comrades and our kin of our age. I had been away and gone a full handful of years, and I returned and sat beneath the tree upon a seat made by an out-thrust of rootburl. There I sat and long I sat and many passed but none were of our old company. And then came one whose shape I knew, whose walk I knew, even before I kenned his face.

"It was Orfas.

"He came and I remembered it was right that I should rise because he was my father's brother of the half-blood, and so we at some length stood and faced each other. He had the slight semblance of a smile on his face. For a while we said no word. And then I said, 'It seems, then, that of all only we two remain, in this corner of the Land of Thule.'

"And he said, 'It seems that this be one too many,' and although I did not deeply consider on his words, still, a parti-cle of them must have touched upon a particle in me—at once I said, 'Then let us both be gone and let us make a compact and both be gone together.' We made our compact and prepared a boat and formed an alliance with others, gathered our gear and store and had the witcherers discover the best day to depart. South-south across the all-encircling sea we went, to the barbar-lands we made our course, sometimes along the coast and sometimes up the great rivers. Betimes we traded and betimes we sold the service of our swords and spears, fighting now for one town or tribe or chieftan, now for another; and betimes we shared the plunder-spoil or betimes we kept it all, as it had been agreed, or as it fell out. And then for a while we went a-roving and a-robbing as we would and as we willed, until the durancy of our compact fell away to expire, and there was only a handful of day-sticks left in the tally-bag. One of us had a dream to take a certain course with our three vessels (as by then they were) and reach on the third day an island all suitable for our needs, which was done, and the day we broke the third stick we made our landfall and the island was as had been seen."

~ ~ ~ ~ ~

EVERYONE has in his mind the image presented by story and by song, of all the troves and treasures piled in one great glittery heap, "dragon-high, dragon-bright, sparkling while its seekers fight—" but it is not always thus in fact, nor was it so this time.

Said he who had dreamed the dream, "Think it clearly for yourselves. Will he who lives alone to claim it be wanting to lug it all back to the ships again?" There was a burst of laughter in which was no sound of love or warmth. It was done so, that the wealth was divided between two ships, which were dismasted, and the third was broken up at once to make a deck for the complete vessel, which was a double-hulled raft of sorts, with a single mast. Then each man set to sharpening his weapons and mostly he sat alone, with no more than now and then a sideways glance to estimate the strength or calculate the skill of another; and sometimes the other, on whom his direct look might fall had been his near-comrade; and some seemed to repent greatly of this compact and to wish themselves away.

But only one would live to go away.

The fighting field was laid out and deeply trenched around, and then the lots were drawn to select the two for the first combat. Orfas drew one of the black pebbles and a younger man, often a singer of merry songs, drew the other. He sang no song now but muttered charms as they stepped to the center of the field but Orfas did not open his mouth as they faced each other. Then all the rest shouted *Ho!* and in that instant Orfas spat in his opponent's eye and as he blinked, dumbstruck, Orfas rushed him from the side of that eye and with his axe he split through his collarbone. The man fell backward with a great croaking cry. Orfas kicked up the fallen one's kilt and again he spat, now upon his foe's manhood, saying, "That is for the wench you stole of me a two months' since!" and then he brought the axe down once again.

And went and took his rest across the trench until every other man should have fought once—and then he would again be subject to the lots.

Not every victor lived to draw a second lot.

Now—said Arntat—I had killed my man and had killed my second man. And as I sat resting and waiting I chanced to feel an eye strong upon me and I looked up and around and I saw that it was the eye of Orfas. It came to me that I had felt it heavy upon me before but had not fully thought about it. And now all at once I recollected what had been said that time we met after long apart, under the tree of meeting; I saying, *It seems that only we two remain*, and he saying, *This be one too many*. It came to me so late as then that he had long hated me, and I suppose that inside me that one particle must have returned his feeling or I would not have answered as I did.

Well! So be it! I knew then that we two would be the last to stand upon our feet and fight for life and for treasure, winner take all. It was our weird. I do not know at what point in our lives he had begun to hate me—or why. Perhaps he himself did not know it till he saw me there under the tree of meeting. Perhaps until then he had thought I would not come back, that I was dead; it may be that the deaths of others of our line had gradually or suddenly given him hope that he would be chief over all our line—and, as our line has always been a line high in Thule, he may have bethought him that he might some day be highest of all in Thule.

If I were not.

~ ~ ~ ~ ~

THE fire barely lived at all. Then someone blew briefly on the dull embers and someone placed an armful of bracken on it. "Eh, ah, Bear," an older nain said. "Well I remember when the old asking began to be heard again. *By what three things is a king made?* and answered, *By strength, by magic, and by fortune.* He who paid the nain-fee then, I shall say plain, was not the worst as ever paid it. But even kings live not forever. And in all that struggle which came then, Bear, some say thee helped the Orfas, he being near of kin. Some say thee befoed him and would have been king instead. I ask not and care I not. Thee has ever been the friend of nains, as nains have ever been the friends of thee. The Orfas winned the kingship and was made king as kings be made and he paid the nain-fee—*then*—full and fair. But the nains be feed to work in iron, not to set snares for bears—or men. We saw thee in the wildwood dwelling where never manfolk dwell at all, we told it to each other and we told it to the forge, but never did we tell it to the king."

"I know."

"Such rewards he offered, and such afflictions he threatened as never did we hear before."

"I know."

"That bitter winter when the birds fell frozen from the sky and the all-circling sea itself was turned to ice, far as ever eye could see, when no track nor trace could be concealed upon the snowy ground and no snow fell more from the fast frozen sky; then the Orfas came for thee, for Witch-Mered did plot it out for him."

"I know."

"Corby-Mered. Mered-Crow."

"His witcheries espied thee out, we knew and said nought, he saw and said all. With a many troops of men they came for thee, and circled around where thee had gone. Where could thee hide? We thought it woe, we whispered low, we told it to the forge, but nains mix not in the affairs of man-folk—would that man would mix as little in the life of nain-folk! They circled all about where thee had gone, they scanned the still, unbroken snow, they drew their lines in-ward as wading fishermen draw their nets, they met face to face and arm to arm in the center; but *Arn* they never met."

"I know."

He said, "I know. I know." Crouching in the darkness marred by feebleflicks of flames, he said, "I cannot forget." A prisoner, he remembered himself a fugitive; though it had seemed bitter then, now long later it revealed its sweetnesses. And he could not forget.

The nains sighed and they sighed for him, not for them-selves. The king had sought him then and found him not, and hunted him again and found him not. King and king's men hunted a man, but he whom they hunted was a man no more. He had become a bear.

VII

DAY FOLLOWED DAY and toil followed toil and slowly the
great rust increased. Its pace was not steady. At times it had
seemed to leap onward like a dread grass fire in the dry season, at times it had seemed to pause as though tired. Now for
some long while, the redsickness had gone at so slow a step
that some did not perceive that it still continued until, perhaps, an axe-head crumbled as it met the wood it could not
cleave, or an arrowhead collapsed into a pinch of russet dust
when the quiver was moved. And many still had not realized
that the pest pursued its course.

But the king was not among the many.

It was not only that he asked or caused to be asked, "How
goes it with iron?" of those who came from far off. He asked
always, in hope of hearing what he would hear; but he was
not content only to ask. The king had great store of iron, not
in the armories alone, but in his own chambers, very near to
him. Several times a day, if he did not go to iron things, he
had iron things come to him. He looked, he tested, poked,
probed, he scraped iron with his fingernails and he scaled
with instruments which were not of iron. The king knew the
rate each day at which the plague pursued. He knew it and he
sickened from his knowing.

"Will you not leave off?" the queen asked him with a
sigh.

"How can I?" he asked, with a sick and sidelong look.

There was almost a proverb in those days: *The queen
grows not old.* Some had grown up hearing it and thought it a
saying applied to all queens; that women who held the
queenly seat, by virtue of the power of that office did not
age. But in truth it was a saying which had not been heard
before, although likely enough that any woman spared the
labors of hoeing and bark-beating and preparing hides and all
such toilsome work, who had but to put on her clothes and
jewelry and suckle her children—and sometimes not even
such slight, light tasks as that—likely enough that thus a

woman, queen or not, would grow not old so soon and certain as the generality of her sex.

Still, the saying was a new one, as sayings go. Here lies the truth—quite early had her hair turned the color of a winter's sky, quite early and quite suddenly. Therefore most of Thule became aware of her when she in some measure already wore the mantle of more years than she had. And also her manner had already then become grave and withdrawn. Since the mass of folk did not observe her slowly losing what were common tokens of youth, gradually the saying came to be heard: *The queen grows not old.*

Some held this to be due to her command of witchery-wisdom. Only a few, and they not often and never openly, were lately beginning to whisper that she sipped the cup of the king's own years, that she stayed one age while he aged swiftly. And at least the very last part of this was true.

"You can leave off by leaving off," she said. Only a very few lines were to be seen upon her face—about the eyes, and about the corners of the mouth—but none at all upon her upper lip. "Rest upon your cot or couch and let others examine iron while you watch. And watch not too closely, that is to say, too nearly. Iron is sorely ill. And you are not too well."

A slight snarl moved his mouth, but did not move it much; his next words and the inclination of his head showed how little the snarl was meant for her. "You are ever gentle of me in word and deed—but I know well what they say out *there*—that I have caught the ironrot. Perhaps I have. But if I have caught it, I have it—so what good then be distance? Or any precaution?" He moved nonetheless to his couch. Muttered, "If iron die, then I die. If I die, let iron die. But let we not die, either, nor the barbar folk come swarming—savages from over the circling sea—" He let himself down on his couch and leaned on the pile of prime pelts sewn in bags and stuffed with the downy breast feathers of swans. His eyes were sunken and closed. A long breath shuddered and sighed in his throat and fluttered his cracked and blistered lips.

Suddenly his eyes flew open. Those of the queen were fixed upon his. "Why do you think he came back alone? Or did he?" Without giving her time to reply he rolled his head back and forth and clenched his hands. "Only because Mered-delfin feels that this traitor may somehow prove the key to the cure of iron do I spare his life." His teeth showed and sounded. "I should never have spared it before." Another thought worked its way across his ravaged face and the queen drew near and kneeled beside him. "Mered-delfin—he said that you must prepare to wear many masks and to make many journeys." She gave a slow, single nod. The king said, "Wear one mask now. Make one short journey."

~ ~ ~ ~ ~

FROM time to time word came, presumably from the king, to switch the mining from the open pit to the tunnels or from the tunnels to the open pit. Evidently neither change had perceptibly improved the fate of iron, but from time to time still came directions—*change*.

Thus on this day the mattocks swung up and down upon the encircling path which went around and around about the great deep pit, up from its narrow center to its wider rim, digging deeper into the walls of ruddy ore. *Up* the tools went, paused, still scattering dust; *down* they fell, a grunt, a thud, and some were of bone and some were of stone, but none were of iron. Arnten had been detailed to carry the yoke with its brace of leathern water buckets and a drinking horn slung about his neck on a thong. For the most part he kept his eyes on the uneven footing of the circling path, but when he paused to allow one of the nain-thralls to drink he allowed himself to look up. The yoke had bitten into his flesh, but he preferred it out here in the open pit. He thought they all must. It was like being inside a great clay pot, one only partly made; the pot-woman had rolled the strip of red clay between her palms and coiled it into the rough shape of the pot-to-be, but she had not yet taken up her shell or shard to smooth it. The pit was like a great clay pot and they were inside it, small as mandrakes.

Of course, pots had no light blue lids on them. Against the rim, outlined, stood the guards. His eyes swung around. The nain groaned gratefully between gulps. All about the rim the guards stood at equal intervals, weapons sticking up like fishnet sticks. But at one place there were a number of them grouped together. They moved and he saw that one of them had no spear, no club, seemed to be dressed differently. Dressed more.

The nain gave one last groan, looked enviously at the rest of the water in the pails, licked his mouth and bristles and put the flat of his huge hand between the boy's shoulders below the yoke the nain had effortlessly lifted into place, gently shoved him on his way. The yoke grew lighter as he went from nain to nain. Presently he stood before his father. Arntat looked at him a moment with a dull gaze. His eyes were filmy. Then they saw the boy. A faint smile rested briefly on his haggard face. Suddenly the boy cried out, "I am sorry! I am sorry, Father, that I ever took away the bearskin!"

The yoke was lifted, the buckets put down. "I had set all things to *that* end," his father said. "As for all *this*—it be our weird. Ah, water. Good." He took the horn and dipped it full and raised his head as he raised the horn to his mouth and his eyes settled on something beyond. For a moment he did not move. Then his teeth clicked and rattled on the rim of the horn. Then he made sounds in his throat. And next he drank. But his eyes never moved.

A guard, perhaps thinking that they had been too long over the matter, approached—the expression on his face was part sneer and part fear. He gave a quick look over his shoulder and with his head motioned to another guard to follow. This first guard set his features for stern speech and gave the hand which held the club a shake or two. But what he was about to say went unsaid, as from above and beyond a voice whose syllables the boy could not make out came floating on the air and echoed twice or more. The guard's face twisted in his own effort to comprehend, then showed surprise—regret—relief. The guard turned away, turned back, spoke to the guard behind. And this one gave a quick look at the captive father and son, a quick look up and beyond. He shrugged. The two king's men moved apart and drew themselves up in a stance of bravado and watchfulness.

Arntat let out a long breath. One hand groped for his son. The other then hung the horn-thong around the boy's neck. A drop of water trickled from it, made a muddy wormtrack through the dust on his chest. Both hands found the yoke and lifted it as the boy bent to receive it. Both hands turned the boy around and told him, plain as words, to be on his way. Arnten went. He went several steps. He heard behind him the grunt and the thud as, rest over, toil returned to, the mattock struck the red-ore ground. Then he stopped and looked up, whither his father had looked, up to where the guards had looked. Nothing was there. His eyes, darting about, saw again the group of guards. They had just begun crossing over the rim and, as one by one they stepped out of sight, he saw once more the unarmed person among them, who paused upon the edge between earth and sky. Pausing for a moment and looking back, this person for an instant seemed to have raised wings poised for flight.

Wide-cut sleeves. A woman.

She vanished over the rim.

A blow caught him in the ribs, a rock fell and bounced. He dodged the second. It came from the guard who had desisted from striking him and his father before. But he had to move and turn his back and yet balance the yoke and the buckets, so he could not run. The third stone caught him. And so did the fourth.

~ ~ ~ ~ ~

WHEN the thralls lay down their mattocks and began to load the broken ore into the barrows the first captain looked, saying nothing. Afterward he gestured to Arnten and Arntat. "You two—or you one and half—" the guards guffawed— "Take the tools to the tunnel. The rest of you to the forge." Two by two, the nains stooped and took up the barrow poles. Low at first like a mutter, then a rumble, as though the voices had descended from mouth to throat and chest; then so very high it seemed almost that they sang not at all as they padded along the curving path—and then cry after cry, as great wave after great wave breaking upon the rocks—

> *The swans fly overhead*
> *And the nains see them.*
> *The moles tunnel through the earth*
> *And the nains see them.*

The guards could not ken the words, but the sound of the chant made them uneasy. They howled and mocked, they threw stones, small ones but vicious and thrown hard.

> *The king's fire gives no light,*
> *The queen's light gives no fire,*
> *Evil, evil, are these times,*
> *These carrion times, consumed by crows.*
> *When will the wizard's mouths be fed,*
> *And the nains see it?*

The tools were gathered and bundled together like great faggots of firewood. Father and son bowed their backs beneath their loads and turned their faces toward the tunnel. It was not the load that made Arntat tremble now, nor was it his last labor of the day that made him sweat and gasp. Unwilling, unwilling, slow, were his steps and he craned his neck at the darkening sky as though he would never see it again.

Beyond them the guards seemed to have been taken by a frenzy, stoning the nains and shouting and feinting at them with clubs and spears. But above all such noise the wild chant continued to be heard.

> *The king's evil rots like rust,*
> *And the nains see it.*
> *When will the stars throw down their spears,*
> *And the nains see it?*
> *Then may this kingdom turn to dust,*
> *And the nains see it!*

~ ~ ~ ~ ~

SOMETIMES the bigger Arn trudged back and forth in the
tunnel, head stooped low—perhaps for safety, perhaps from
apathy—hands against the sides as though at any moment he
might push one or another of them aside. Sometimes he
shambled on all his limbs, head weaving from side to side.
But he was sitting motionless when the dry bracken rustled
as it sometimes did, as though remembering when it was
alive and yielding to each slight breeze. And a woman came
in. She first saw the smaller Arn, and for just a moment the
smooth composure of her face was disturbed—how curious,
then, her expression! He moved at once to his father's side
and her face was as before. In a single motion, effortless,
graceful, she seated herself, her legs tucked under, her hands
resting in her lap. Son looked at father and he thought his
father looked as though he had always been looking at her.

"Yet another son gotten, Ahazmazra," she said. "And so
much younger than the others." She made a slight sound as if
pleasantly relaxing from some not too onerous task and she
said, "You will want to know about your other sons."

Lips barely moving, he said, "Either they died or they
made their peace. I can do them no good. Nor they me."

Calmly: "You may do good for this one then," she said.

This one, crouching next to his father, was not much
thinking how good could be done for him. Part of his mind
was entranced by the appearance of her. Part of his mind
scurried and searched, as a squirrel rousting nuts, for certain
words his father had said—when? Long, long ago. When
they were free.

'Tis nought to you what's my-name-then. But now he
knew, his fullfather's name then was Ahazmazra and if this
woman knew it she had known him then. Her underdress,
beneath which her feet were tucked, was all of blue. He had
never seen so much cloth of blue before, blue was a precious
color, a sky-color, and he had heard more than one say that
far-far-away at the farthermost edge of the world dwelt the
Sky Gatherers and that all the blue in the world came from
them, scarce, scarce, precious and beautiful blue: but his old
uncle had said this was in no way true and that blue was

made from an herb called woad; it did not flourish in Thule, was brought from the barbar-lands and traded for amber, weight for weight.

Ahaz-mazra. And not Arn.

My other begotten sons . . . made upon empty bearhide in lawful bedchamber. Her sleeveless overdress was the whitest white which he had ever seen, paler than the common pallor of bark-cloth, and came to her knees. Round yoke and hem were broad and complex broider-work in several colors, flowers and leaves and thicket—something else which he could not quite determine and which peered out of the thicket. Around her neck was a rope of pieces of amber wrapped in golden wire. Her face was strong, serious, totally self-assured. Although she had come from the free, the outside world, she had come neither to triumph nor to condescend. *I have dabbled.* Why was that word in his mind? . . . *have dabbled . . .* Or should it be *dappled?* That made no sense. Yet the memory that went with the words was of his father's face dappled by a leaf shadows as he held for a passing moment a branch he presently threw upon the fire. *I have—*

"I have done ill enough for him by getting him," said his father (now) to the strange woman. Who said a strange, strange thing indeed.

"You may get him back with you whither you both came—on a ship already prepared in all things—at dawn tide three days hence," she said. "You have only to renounce the curse on iron and to swear by your shadow and by his that it shall stay renounced. And you may even delay compliance to the last—when the third day's sun comes up and shadows first appear—upon the very shore beside the ship."

The sick, confused look, which had been absent since her entrance, now returned to the man's face. He muttered, uncertainly. "The third day's sun?"

"It is three days' journey to where the boats are."

He squinted, trying to resolve all into sense. Then he in one swift rush was on his feet and Arnten cried out and put his hands on his own head as though feeling the pain of his father's would crash upon the tunnel top. But that one or two fingers' breadth away the man's head stayed, stooped. The woman had not moved. She did not even raise her eyes. And the man fell to a charging position, his eyes level with hers, his face very close to hers, his eyes now suffused with blood.

"Innahat—erex," he cried, "ah, eh! Does that crow still live, that he has stolen all the wits of thee? 'Wither we both came?' 'By ship?' 'Renounce the curse on iron?' What babblement is this? From nowhere did we come by ship! No word of any curse on iron heard I ever till my cub here did mention it, before we fell into the nets of your long-tongued lord! 'Sear by my shadow and by his?' Eh, ah! By my shadow and by his, then—"

~ ~ ~ ~ ~

MORE than once, after having returned in from out, Arnten had felt sickened and dizzied. The sun might have been the cause, beating as it did on him all day. Such a moment came upon him suddenly as he wondered what great oath his father was about to swear upon their twain shadows. He closed his eyes. He did not hear if the oath were sworn. He did hear the distant droning of the nains as they returned, as their voices rose suddenly and dropped again. The strange woman was now gone, he saw. He saw his father's eyes were fixed on his and all manner of strange things he saw in them.

"Eh, ah, Bear! What odd thing we seed by yonder tunnel-mouth but two, or three! How 't did leap! A hare! Was 'tan omen, eh?"

"I ken't not, if omen 'tiz," another nain said. "But 'twas as thee say, senior Aar-heved-heved-aar, a great puss-longears indeed, and would I'd a snare to catch she doe-hare, do she return—eh?—cub?"

For this other nain looked now at Arnten, who had stood up, although still dizzied, waving his hand, trying frantically to put a thought into words before the thought fled. "The hare came in!" he said, almost stammering. "The hare came in! What way she came in, would she not go out?"

The man put an arm around his son. The comforting nain-drone and nain musk surrounded them. The boy's head drooped upon his father's side. He felt weak and sore and hungry. Food would come. Words sang in his head and faint fires danced there. *Bee and salmon, wolf and bear.* A rough hand rested gently on him. *Tiger, lion, male and hare.*

Fetters do not bind the moles.

And the nains see them.

VIII

AAR-heved-heved-aar that night sent a youngster nain to search out the passage where the hare had run. Guards did not trust the lower levels at night, would not even if the nains were gone. Posts and watch fires were at pit mouth only. Even wind and rain could not drive the guards more than a few feet inside after full dark. The nain-senior knew this, but did not trust the slickskins as cowards any more than he trusted them as braves; he chose to lessen all risks. It was not true that nains had full vision in the dark, but in this wise their eyes were in between those of men and those of beasts. The younger nain reported that although the tunnel appeared to be a blind gut, yet it did not end clean. A huge pile of debris at one end seemed to show that it might not always have been a blind gut—that perhaps the roof had fallen in at one time. And, more than this, the younger nain had sought and found the scent of the hare and it had seemed to go on up the pile of detritus to its peak.

"But I clambered not after it," he concluded.

"Wisely," said the senior. "For though I be as much a-zeal as any to be gone from here, needless risks we must not take. It is man who is impetuous, but we nains do be deliberate, so—"

"Feed the wizards."

Aar-heved-heved-aar, true to his penultimate word, reflected. Then, "Eh, ah, Bear. Say thee well."

"Feed the wizards!"

The nain-senior looked up at the man—for all his breadth, the nain was no taller than Arnten—and nodded his massive head. "That must be our aim, hard task though it be. It is the coming death of iron which has turned this king's head mad and turned his hands against us all. His need be great. But is our need not greater? If he do die tonight and tomorrow we be told that we be free, what then? Iron be our life, without iron we be dead nains. 'Tiz but the first step, getting gone from here. He will pursue we, but if he should not, what, eh? We do make the hoe, but we hoe not; we have traded iron and iron's work for most our food. We make the spearhead, but we cast no spear. And if we will to eat in the woods, as the wild brawnes do—say, ah!—be not the wild brawnes a fitter match for us, be we not armed with iron?"

He uttered a long, shuddering cry and his head shook so from side to side that his thick hair rustled upon his broad and shaggy shoulders. "Men gender much," he said, "and the men-wives bear often. Nains gender seldom for our passion be for the forge and few are the nain-bairns our shes do get. Before the Great Bear took starfire and gave it we and be-teached we how to delve and deliver metal from the earth's belly and to mold and shape it as the bears do mold and shape their cubs—before even the yore-tide—men were few and nains were few and lived they twain folk far apart, for broad and long be Thule.

"But since then men have swarmed—yet the nain's num-bers do stay the same. Still be Nainland far from menland, eh but ah, *it be not so far as once 'twas!* Men can hunt without iron, men can farm without iron, men can still beget them many mennikins without iron; men can do without iron and I betell thee this: *If men may live without iron, men may live without nains.*"

The echo of his voice was long in his listeners' minds.

He divided them into nine watches and to each watch he assigned a third part of one night. And the first watch for the first third of the first night began at once to clear away with slow care the rubble at the end of what they had begun to call The Doe-Hare's Den. The nains stripped off their leather kilts and piled loose stone therein, then gathered up the corners four and slung the juried bags over their shoulders and trudged away on noiseless feet to empty their loads well out of sight in yet another disused corridor. And then to return. Thus, while the work went on, none lost more rest than one-third of every third night; and, after many nights, the toilers in the Doe-Hare's Den, pausing a moment for rest, recognized in their nostrils the bitter, faint, familiar smell of woodsmoke—and recognized that an aperture, of whatsoever a nature, existed between them in their captivity and the unfettered outside world.

~ ~ ~ ~ ~

AND thus the elusive memory returned to the boy. Remembering woodsmoke and firelight and father's words, he said, "The strange woman who was here. Was she the queen of love with whom you dabbled and dallied?"

A silence. "Eh, she was."

"Be that why the king do hate thee?"

A growl. "She said he never knew."

"Then why *do* he hate thee?"

A grunt. "Has thee forgot my tale of how he and me vowed a compact and at the end stood face to face to fight for treasure and for life, winner take all?"

"No, I remember that."

A cough. A second, longer, deeper cough.

A gasp. "I won. He lay at my feet. He groveled and gibbered. I raised him up, gave him half the plunder and I spared his life. That is why. For this he cannot forgive me."

~ ~ ~ ~ ~

IN THE darkness he heard droning of dry and dusty voices and he knew it was the wizards that he heard. He heard them droning as though ineffably bored and weary, as though repeating over and over to themselves, lest they forget, forcing their dust-choked voices and thinking with dust-choked minds, at a great distance away, repeating something of great importance which must not be forgotten— *The bear dies, iron dies. The bear dies, iron dies. As the bear comes to life, so must iron come to life. As the bear comes to life, so must iron come to life.* A pause, a faint gasp, the click of voices in dry, dusty throats. And again and again the droning recommenced. *The bear sleeps in the ground, so must iron sleep in the ground. As the bear sleeps its death-sleep-life, so must iron . . .*

The bear dies, iron dies . . .

Endlessly he heard this. The sound ebbed and faded away as he felt himself gently rocked.

"What?"

"Bear's boy, it be time."

Time for iron, time for . . . But the droning voices were away and gone. Had he heard them echoing thinly in a cavern somewhere? Or was it only the familiar echo of the nain voices in the mine? Confused, already forgetting, he got up.

Still half asleep he followed, sometimes stumbling, as the men filed from their sleeping-cell into unguarded tunnels. In the Doe-Hare's Hole he saw the now familiar sight of and heard the now familiar sounds of debris and detritus being shoveled and scraped into the carrying-skins. But while this still went on he heard those who watched and who waited discussing whither they should go when they had made their escape from the mines: and should they go in one body for defense, or should they split up and make their several—or it might be their many—ways, in order to divide and so to weaken their pursuers.

He did not hear if an answer had been concluded, let alone what it was, for Aar-heved-heved-aar took hold of him and said, "Bear's-boy, 'tis thought they have broke through up ahead. Get thee up then, for thee be but small as be compare to us and maybe can find out—"

The senior nain did not finish his phrase, but propelled Arnten forward, saying, "Up, then, and up and up."

Though so much diminished, still the pile was high and required climbing. He half scuttled and he half slid as he set to climbing. And he had somehow a fear that, though he went on his way slow enough, still, he might strike his head there in the darkness; and from this fear he went slower. And every few paces he paused and thrust his hands forward.

And by and by he felt his hand as it scraped the face of the cavern suddenly fall through into nothingness, and he fell forward a bit and he grunted rather than cried out. And ahead of him, where yet he could not see, ahead of him in the black, black, blackness, something moved which was even blacker (though how he knew this he did not know). Something made a sudden movement and a sudden noise and he had the impression that something had been waiting and hearkening, listening very closely, he had an impression of a head cocked to one side—

And before he himself could do more, the sound from the other side of the hole ceased to be startled, flurried, resolved itself into the flap of wings in the darkness.

And he and all of them heard the sudden sharp cry of a crow. And again, farther away. And once more, faint.

~ ~ ~ ~ ~

Now the work quickened, concentrated and focused on enlarging the opening. An opening onto the world at large? Or into another cave? If the latter, still, this next cave must itself open onto the world at large, else how came any bird to be there? But the stone or bone blades of their picks no longer sank into rubble. Either they sprang back as they were swung against the lips of the scrape-hole or they shattered. The nains began to mutter. Then Arn came forward on all fours, reached out his long, shaggy arms, felt and pawed and groped in the darkness.

"It seems that two slabs of rock all but meet face to face here," he said. "Some bit of softer stone did rest between them, as might a piece of stale bread between a dead man's teeth—

"Now, part of that had weathered away, else that hare had neither entered nor left—and we have battered away the rest—but the teeth be fixed firm. Somehow we must crack the jawbones, then. So—"

His voice fell into a muttering growl.

"We must break the jaws of the rock," he said once more. "How?" he muttered. "How? *How?*"

~ ~ ~ ~ ~

A DULL glow from a brazier of coals made shadows as the king moved slowly and painfully upon his bed. Something scuttled outside the chamber. Someone entered on hands and knees. The king lifted his head, stopped, groaned, rubbed his face, moaned.

"You smell of mold and of trees," he whispered. "Well—what?"

Merred-delphin panted a moment. Then: "Slayer of—"

The king made a noise of loathing, deep in his throat.

"Damn all fulsome phrases! None's here now save thee and me. *What?*"

"Wolf—the mine-thralls—trying to break—" His wind failed, his voice caught in his scrannel chest and throat.

His master finished the words. "To break out? Eh? To—" He struggled up, hissed his pain, rested on his elbows. Raised his voice. "*Hoy!*" he cried. "The captain of the guard! *Hoy! Hoy!* Hither! Flay him, does he slumber? Hither! Here! Now! *Hoy!*"

~ ~ ~ ~ ~

THE bear half-slid, half-crawled backward. The air in the hole was thick. "Bring bracken," he said. "Bring all the bracken that be. Not all of ye!" he called sharply. "The crew of the first third—go!" What might have been confusion was at once averted. "The crew of the second third—to that line of tunnel where the pit props be fallen and bring, for the first fetch, the smallest and the softest pieces of the dry-rotted old props—"

He waited till they had got them gone and next he said, "Senior Aar. We must needs soon make fire."

A moment, then the elder nain murmured, "Ah, bear, that be no easy thing, thee knows."

"I do know!"

"They take care—and always have—the accursed smoothskins, that we have no flint about us—to name but one lack—and though we might break the pick-handles, their wood be not—"

"And this, all this, I know. And *thee* knows and all of ye know what I mean. Well. The cub and I will withdraw."

Softly, as it might have been reluctantly, the senior nain said, "Nay the twain of ye may bide. 'Tis no time to stand upon custom."

He made a sign to the remaining nains and, though somewhat slowly, they joined hands. There was scarce room even at the broader end of the Doe-Hare's cave for a wide circle, shoulder to broad shoulder they stood, hand in hand, leg against leg and foot against foot. All was silent and, as silence will when thought upon, silence gradually gave voice. Silence whispered to itself, and silence began to sing a little song. It was a curious bit of song and it hissed and it crackled as the nain feet shuffled, as the nain forms shifted themselves in the darkness, as the small and cramped circle went around and around in the darkness, softly stamping feet upon the rubble-strewn floor.

Arnten stared into the blackness and, as it will when stared long into, the blackness began to give light, a faint blue light, a spark, a worm, a glow that had no outline and faded. And then did not fade.

Arnten felt the hairs on his flesh rise as his skin puckered in something the far side of fear. He saw in the darkness the forms of the nains and he saw their hairs risen and he saw upon that nimbus of hair outlining each head and each body a nimbus of blue light: and as the nains so softly-softly muttered the lights wavered and as the nains slowly circled around the blue lights slowly undulated and as the nains slowly and softly stamped their feet the blue lights softly hissed and softly crackled.

The dance did not cease when the first crew returned, arms laden with the great coarse bracken-fern; Arnten gestured and they passed their burdens, bundle by bundle, to the end of the cave. First they stuffed it through the still small opening into the outside world and then, when this would take no more, piled it all around about.

Then the second crew began to come back, stripped to the buff, their garment-skins used as carryalls for piles of wood from the fallen pit-props, soft from long dry rot, and Arnten gestured again and they piled wood on the bracken. And still the slow, strange dance went on and on. Arn, in a few words, bade two more crews begone. They must bring back the larger stumps and shafts of the wooden columns used here and there to hold up the tunnel roof.

The dancing nains, meanwhile, had danced nearer and closer to what was now a bosky mass of dry-rotted wood and bracken. The dancing nains were pressed together almost as though to make one enormous grotesque creature with many limbs, a sort of nainipede; and this grotesque heaved and huddled close to the piled up bracken-fern which had been its bed. Still it sang and still the blue lights wavered at the ends of its hairs; and then the blue light gathered itself together into one mass and the nainipede went dancing back on its many limbs. The ball of light floated up and bounced along the rough roof of the cave and settled upon the pile of wood. It seemed next to snuggle and to creep its way deep into the bracken and then there was a flash and the blue was gone and there was the familiar red and orange and yellow of fire. And the song was silent but in its place they heard the crackling of flames.

~ ~ ~ ~ ~

MERRED-DELPHIN stood by the curtained door and flapped wide black sleeves.

"My men have them safe now?" the Orfas demanded.

His chief witcherer opened his mouth and closed it, long thin tongue fluttering. Then he said, "They will not go."

Then seemed the King confused. "How now? Won't go? The nains?"

Merred shook his dry old head, his long nose seeming to point all ways at once. "Not the nains, King Wolf! The men! Your men! The king's men will not go! They will not go down into the mine! It seems—I should have remembered that—" His voice stuck, came out again at last. "They fear the deep, they fear the darkness, assuredly they fear the nains and their witchery."

The old wolf let waste no time in rage and imprecation, but he rubbed one rusty wrist with one rusty hand and he said in the voice of one who thinks, "Then what is it which they may fear e'en more, my crow, than the nains and the deep and dark—eh?"

They looked at each other. The king's eyes went past the old vizier and the old vizier turned; and together they exclaimed a word.

~ ~ ~ ~ ~

SO DRY was bracken and dry-rotted wood that both together burned with minimal smoke, but smoke even so there was. Arn and Arnten and the nains stood in the main corridor and with their garment-skins they flapped and fanned away the smoke. And now and then they stopped and took sips of water from the buckets, but only sips. A thin glow of firelight lit the somber halls of underground and over this overlay a thin haze of smoke. The fire dance of the nainfolk had ceased.

He leaned against his father and in his body he was in the mine-cave and beside his father, yet in his mind he was beside his old uncle in the old man's medicine hut. And there was the sound of a dance . . . the sound of a drum . . .

Out of the dimness and the deep, deep darkness came the figures of men. It was no vision or dream—here, in the mine and out of the darkness of the mine-tunnels, they came.

"The guards," said Aar. "Aye, ehh'ng, be sure, be sure, 'twas that skulk-crow as sped the word to their crank lord." And in the naintongue he said a word. The men came not fast ahead, they moved slowly, irresolute. And in the dim glow of the fire and the thin haze of the smoke the nains began another sort of dance. They moved their feet up and down and they leaned forward and they waved their long, long arms. They did not actually move an ell along the tunnel floor, but in the misty, swimmy light, dim and flickering, it seemed as though they did move, did advance; and the men, moaning, dismayed, retreated.

Then at the edge of his ear Arnten heard the sound which had tapped below the surface, the thin *tap-tap, tump-tump*, of a witchery drum. And the soldiers milled about, cried out in alarm and unease. A spurt of fresh air cleared vision for a moment and a way ahead and now it was Arnten who cried out and a murmur went up. For back, far back, as far back as they could see in the main corridor came a marching column, a marching double column, a dancing double column, of figures which were manlike but were no men, a-waving in their tiny hands the menace of tiny spears.

And the witch-drum beat and the witch-things came and the men cried out and turned and turned.

Said one nain voice, amused and scorning, "Do they come at us with mandrakes, then? Nay'ng! The children o' the forge know a power or two for that."

Swiftly said the elder Aar, " 'Tis not against us that they deploy the mandrakes, 'tis to force on the men o' the king, who know no power, let alone two, for that."

Arn, without one word, picked up one of the water buckets and went straightway into the smoke-filled hole of the hare, pausing a moment at the entrance to pick up a fallen bit of bracken and dip it in the water and crush the dripping frond against his nose and mouth. In a moment came a hissing sound and a cloud of steam rolled out and all firelight was quenched.

But not for long, for torches now made appearances farther down the main corridor. The men, fearing the mandrakes more than the nains, came closer.

Arn emerged, stumbling, seized another bucket and again entered the cave. Again there was a hissing and a sizzling and again a cloud of steam. And a long pause—and Arnten held his breath and feared. And then the bear emerged again.

"The fire be out," he said, low and urgent. "And now it comes time to take these two last buckets of water and toss them on the hot rock. Do they crack well, we may all yet take our leave. And if not—" He shrugged. A huge mass of smoldering bracken was dragged out, picked up, heaved toward the advancing soldiery—who cried out, fell back into the smoke and gloom. And the drums beat and the mandrakes moved.

Now, all at once, all were in the place whence the hare had fled. Somehow there was light, light of a thin gray sort, obscured by steam, by smoke, but light. And Arnten felt the floor hot, hot against his feet and hissed his pain. He saw his father toss one bucket, heard him toss the second. Heard a cracking sound. And a second. Heard the nains give cry to their satisfaction. Heard the almost desperate cries of the king's men as they charged. Heard the sound of spears striking against wall and floor. Heard the sound of spear striking against flesh. Heard his voice raised in a wail as he saw his father stumble upon one knee with one spear into him. Saw Aar-heved-heved-aar fall and saw him crawl and saw him writhe and heard his death rattle.

Saw the bear seizing the very rims of the hole of the rock and smelled his flesh burn and saw his shoulders writhe and saw the rock face crack still more. Cried out and wailed again as he saw his father turn toward him, face grim and hideous and smudged with ash and soot and blood spurting from nose and mouth. Saw that protruding from his father's flesh which he knew was the bloodied head of a spear. Felt his father seize him up and swing him around and protect his smaller body and thrust him through the hole in the rock whence came the milky light of dawn. Felt the last great thrust of that great body and saw the mine vanish from sight and felt the hot rock graze his side and saw the sky and felt himself fall. And roll. And move, crawling, crawling. Leaves in his mouth, dust in his nostrils, smoke all about him. Then no smoke about him. Writhing on his belly like a wounded snake. No more smoke. Shouts and cries in his mind alone. Then silence falling in his mind.

His father.

His father's face.

His father's deed.

At this last moment his father had said no word.

His deed had been enough.

THE END

RAMBLE HOUSE'S

HARRY STEPHEN KEELER WEBWORK MYSTERIES

(RH) indicates the title is available ONLY in the RAMBLE HOUSE edition

The Ace of Spades Murder
The Affair of the Bottled Deuce (RH)
The Amazing Web
The Barking Clock
Behind That Mask
The Book with the Orange Leaves
The Bottle with the Green Wax Seal
The Box from Japan
The Case of the Canny Killer
The Case of the Crazy Corpse (RH)
The Case of the Flying Hands (RH)
The Case of the Ivory Arrow
The Case of the Jeweled Ragpicker
The Case of the Lavender Gripsack
The Case of the Mysterious Moll
The Case of the 16 Beans
The Case of the Transparent Nude (RH)
The Case of the Transposed Legs
The Case of the Two-Headed Idiot (RH)
The Case of the Two Strange Ladies
The Circus Stealers (RH)
Cleopatra's Tears
A Copy of Beowulf (RH)
The Crimson Cube (RH)
The Face of the Man From Saturn
Find the Clock
The Five Silver Buddhas
The 4th King
The Gallows Waits, My Lord! (RH)
The Green Jade Hand
Finger! Finger!
Hangman's Nights (RH)
I, Chameleon (RH)
I Killed Lincoln at 10:13! (RH)
The Iron Ring
The Man Who Changed His Skin (RH)
The Man with the Crimson Box
The Man with the Magic Eardrums
The Man with the Wooden Spectacles
The Marceau Case
The Matilda Hunter Murder
The Monocled Monster

The Murder of London Lew
The Murdered Mathematician
The Mysterious Card (RH)
The Mysterious Ivory Ball of Wong Shing Li (RH)
The Mystery of the Fiddling Cracksman
The Peacock Fan
The Photo of Lady X (RH)
The Portrait of Jirjohn Cobb
Report on Vanessa Hewstone (RH)
Riddle of the Travelling Skull
Riddle of the Wooden Parrakeet (RH)
The Scarlet Mummy (RH)
The Search for X-Y-Z
The Sharkskin Book
Sing Sing Nights
The Six From Nowhere (RH)
The Skull of the Waltzing Clown
The Spectacles of Mr. Cagliostro
Stand By—London Calling!
The Steeltown Strangler
The Stolen Gravestone (RH)
Strange Journey (RH)
The Strange Will
The Straw Hat Murders (RH)
The Street of 1000 Eyes (RH)
Thieves' Nights
Three Novellos (RH)
The Tiger Snake
The Trap (RH)
Vagabond Nights (Defrauded Yeggman)
Vagabond Nights 2 (10 Hours)
The Vanishing Gold Truck
The Voice of the Seven Sparrows
The Washington Square Enigma
When Thief Meets Thief
The White Circle (RH)
The Wonderful Scheme of Mr. Christopher Thorne
X. Jones—of Scotland Yard
Y. Cheung, Business Detective

Keeler Related Works

A To Izzard: A Harry Stephen Keeler Companion by Fender Tucker — Articles and stories about Harry, by Harry, and in his style. Included is a compleat bibliography.

Wild About Harry: Reviews of Keeler Novels — Edited by Richard Polt & Fender Tucker — 22 reviews of works by Harry Stephen Keeler from *Keeler News*. A perfect introduction to the author.

The Keeler Keyhole Collection: Annotated newsletter rants from Harry Stephen Keeler, edited by Francis M. Nevins. Over 400 pages of incredibly personal Keeleriana.

Fakealoo — Pastiches of the style of Harry Stephen Keeler by selected demented members of the HSK Society. Updated every year with the new winner.

Strands of the Web: Short Stories of Harry Stephen Keeler — 29 stories, just about all that Keeler wrote, are edited and introduced by Fred Cleaver.

RAMBLE HOUSE's Loon Sanctuary

A Clear Path to Cross — Sharon Knowles short mystery stories by Ed Lynskey.

A Corpse Walks in Brooklyn and Other Stories — Volume 5 in the Day Keene in the Detective Pulps series.

A Jimmy Starr Omnibus — Three 40s novels by Jimmy Starr.

A Niche in Time and Other Stories — Classic SF by William F. Temple

A Roland Daniel Double: The Signal and The Return of Wu Fang — Classic thrillers from the 30s.

A Shot Rang Out — Three decades of reviews and articles by today's Anthony Boucher, Jon Breen. An essential book for any mystery lover's library.

A Smell of Smoke — A 1951 English countryside thriller by Miles Burton.

A Snark Selection — Lewis Carroll's *The Hunting of the Snark* with two Snarkian chapters by Harry Stephen Keeler — Illustrated by Gavin L. O'Keefe.

A Young Man's Heart — A forgotten early classic by Cornell Woolrich.

Alexander Laing Novels — *The Motives of Nicholas Holtz* and *Dr. Scarlett*, stories of medical mayhem and intrigue from the 30s.

An Angel in the Street — Modern hardboiled noir by Peter Genovese.

Automaton — Brilliant treatise on robotics: 1928-style! By H. Stafford Hatfield.

Away From the Here and Now — Clare Winger Harris stories, collected by Richard A. Lupoff

Beast or Man? — A 1930 novel of racism and horror by Sean M'Guire. Introduced by John Pelan.

Black Beadle — A 1939 thriller by E.C.R. Lorac.

Black Hogan Strikes Again — Australia's Peter Renwick pens a tale of the 30s outback.

Black River Falls — Suspense from the master, Ed Gorman.

Blondy's Boy Friend — A snappy 1930 story by Philip Wylie, writing as Leatrice Homesley.

Blood in a Snap — The *Finnegan's Wake* of the 21st century, by Jim Weiler.

Blood Moon — The first of the Robert Payne series by Ed Gorman.

Bogart '48 — Hollywood action with Bogie by John Stanley and Kenn Davis

Butterfly Man — 1930s novel by Lew Levenson about a dancer who must come to terms with his homosexuality.

Calling Lou Largo! — Two Lou Largo novels by William Ard.

Cathedral of Horror — First volume of collected stories by weird fiction writer Arthur J. Burks.

Chalk Face — Curious supernatural murder thriller by Waldo Frank.

Cornucopia of Crime — Francis M. Nevins assembled this huge collection of his writings about crime literature and the people who write it. Essential for any serious mystery library.

Corpse Without Flesh — Strange novel of forensics by George Bruce

Crimson Clown Novels — By Johnston McCulley, author of the Zorro novels, *The Crimson Clown* and *The Crimson Clown Again.*

Dago Red — 22 tales of dark suspense by Bill Pronzini.

Dark Sanctuary — Weird Menace story by H. B. Gregory

David Hume Novels — *Corpses Never Argue, Cemetery First Stop, Make Way for the Mourners, Eternity Here I Come.* 1930s British hardboiled fiction with an attitude.

Dead Man Talks Too Much — Hollywood boozer by Weed Dickenson.

Death in a Bowl — 1930's murder mystery by Raoul Whitfield.

Death Leaves No Card — One of the most unusual murdered-in-the-tub mysteries you'll ever read. By Miles Burton.

Death March of the Dancing Dolls and Other Stories — Volume Three in the Day Keene in the Detective Pulps series. Introduced by Bill Crider.

Deep Space and other Stories — A collection of SF gems by Richard A. Lupoff.

Detective Duff Unravels It — Episodic mysteries by Harvey O'Higgins.

Devil's Planet — Locked room mystery set on the planet Mars, by Manly Wade Wellman.

Dime Novels: Ramble House's 10-Cent Books — *Knife in the Dark* by Robert Leslie Bellem, *Hot Lead* and *Song of Death* by Ed Earl Repp, *A Hashish House in New York* by H.H. Kane, and five more.

Doctor Arnoldi — Tiffany Thayer's story of the death of death.

Don Diablo: Book of a Lost Film — Two-volume treatment of a western by Paul Landres, with diagrams. Intro by Francis M. Nevins.

Dope and Swastikas — Two strange novels from 1922 by Edmund Snell

Dope Tales #1 — Two dope-riddled classics; *Dope Runners* by Gerald Grantham and *Death Takes the Joystick* by Phillip Condé.

Dope Tales #2 — Two more narco-classics; *The Invisible Hand* by Rex Dark and *The Smokers of Hashish* by Norman Berrow.

Dope Tales #3 — Two enchanting novels of opium by the master, Sax Rohmer. *Dope* and *The Yellow Claw.*

Double Hot — Two 60s softcore sex novels by Morris Hershman.

Double Sex — Yet two more panting thrillers from Morris Hershman.

Dr. Odin — Douglas Newton's 1933 racial potboiler comes back to life.

E. R. Punshon novels — *Information Received, Crossword Mystery, Dictator's Way, Diabolic Candelabra, Music Tells All, Helen Passes By, The House of Godwinsson, The Golden Dagger, Strange Ending, Brought to Light, Dark is the Clue, Triple Quest,* and *Six Were Present*: featuring Bobby Owen.

Ed "Strangler" Lewis: Facts within a Myth — Authoritative illustrated biography of the famous American wrestler Ed Lewis, by noted historian Steve Yohe.

Evangelical Cockroach — Jack Woodford writes about writing.

Evidence in Blue — 1938 mystery by E. Charles Vivian.

Fatal Accident — Murder by automobile, a 1936 mystery by Cecil M. Wills.

Fighting Mad — Todd Robbins' 1922 novel about boxing and life

Five Million in Cash — Gangster thriller by Tiffany Thayer writing as O. B. King.

Food for the Fungus Lady — Collection of weird stories by Ralston Shields, edited and introduced by John Pelan.

Freaks and Fantasies — Eerie tales by Tod Robbins, collaborator of Tod Browning on the film FREAKS.

Gadsby — A lipogram (a novel without the letter E). Ernest Vincent Wright's last work, published in 1939 right before his death.

Gelett Burgess Novels — *The Master of Mysteries, The White Cat, Two O'Clock Courage, Ladies in Boxes, Find the Woman, The Heart Line, The Picaroons* and *Lady Mechante*. Recently added is A Gelett Burgess Sampler, edited by Alfred Jan. All are introduced by Richard A. Lupoff.

Geronimo — S. M. Barrett's 1905 autobiography of a noble American.

Hake Talbot Novels — *Rim of the Pit, The Hangman's Handyman.* Classic locked room mysteries, with mapback covers by Gavin O'Keefe.

Hands Out of Hell and Other Stories — John H. Knox's eerie hallucinations

Hell is a City — William Ard's masterpiece.

Hollywood Dreams — A novel of Tinsel Town and the Depression by Richard O'Brien.

Homicide House — #6 in the Day Keene in the Detective Pulps series.

Hostesses in Hell and Other Stories — Russell Gray's most graphic stories

House of the Restless Dead — Strange and ominous tales by Hugh B. Cave

I Stole $16,000,000 — A true story by cracksman Herbert E. Wilson.

Inclination to Murder — 1966 thriller by New Zealand's Harriet Hunter.

Invaders from the Dark — Classic werewolf tale from Greye La Spina.

J. Poindexter, Colored — Classic satirical black novel by Irvin S. Cobb.

Jack Mann Novels — Strange murder in the English countryside. *Gees' First Case, Nightmare Farm, Grey Shapes, The Ninth Life, The Glass Too Many, Her Ways Are Death, The Kleinert Case* and *Maker of Shadows.*

Jake Hardy — A lusty western tale from Wesley Tallant.

James Corbett — *Vampire of the Skies, The Ghost Plane, Murder Begets Murder* and *The Air Killer* – strange thriller novels from this singular British author.

Jim Harmon Double Novels — *Vixen Hollow/Celluloid Scandal, The Man Who Made Maniacs/Silent Siren, Ape Rape/Wanton Witch, Sex Burns Like Fire/Twist Session, Sudden Lust/Passion Strip, Sin Unlimited/Harlot Master, Twilight Girls/Sex Institution.* Written in the early 60s and never reprinted until now.

J. M. A. Mills — *The Tomb of the Dark Ones* & *Lords of the Earth*: two linked novels involving a group of people battling against occult forces being invoked from Ancient Egypt and Atlantis.

Joel Townsley Rogers Novels and Short Stories — By the author of *The Red Right Hand: Once In a Red Moon, Lady With the Dice, The Stopped Clock, Never Leave My Bed.* Also two short story collections: *Night of Horror* and *Killing Time.*

John Carstairs, Space Detective — Arboreal Sci-fi by Frank Belknap Long

John G. Brandon — *The Case of the Withered Hand, Finger-Prints Never Lie*, and *Death on Delivery*: crime thrillers by Australian author John G. Brandon.

John S. Glasby — Two collections of Glasby's Lovecraftian stories: *The Brooding City* and *Beyond the Rim.* Introduced by John Pelan.

Joseph Shallit Novels — *The Case of the Billion Dollar Body, Lady Don't Die on My Doorstep, Kiss the Killer, Yell Bloody Murder, Take Your Last Look.* One of America's best 50's authors and a favorite of author Bill Pronzini.

Keller Memento — 45 short stories of the amazing and weird by Dr. David Keller.

Killer's Caress — Cary Moran's 1936 hardboiled thriller.

Knowing the Unknowable: Putting Psi to Work — Damien Broderick, PhD puts forward the valid case for evidence of Psi.

Lady of the Yellow Death and Other Stories — More stories by Wyatt Blassingame.

Laughing Death — 1932 Yellow Peril thriller by Walter C. Brown.

League of the Grateful Dead and Other Stories — Volume One in the Day Keene in the Detective Pulps series.

Library of Death — Ghastly tale by Ronald S. L. Harding, introduced by John Pelan

Lords of the Earth — J.M.A. Mills' sequel to *The Tomb of the Dark Ones*, in which the ancient powers of Atlantis are invoked by mere humans.

Mad-Doctor Merciful — Collin Brooks' unsettling novel of medical experimentation with supernatural forces.

Malcolm Jameson Novels and Short Stories — *Astonishing! Astounding!, Tarnished Bomb, The Alien Envoy and Other Stories* and *The Chariots of San Fernando and Other Stories.* All introduced and edited by John Pelan or Richard A. Lupoff.

Man Out of Hell and Other Stories — Volume II of the John H. Knox weird pulps collection.

Marblehead: A Novel of H.P. Lovecraft — A long-lost masterpiece from Richard A. Lupoff. This is the "director's cut", the long version that has never been published before.

Mark of the Laughing Death and Other Stories — Shockers from the pulps by Francis James, introduced by John Pelan.

Master of Souls — Mark Hansom's 1937 shocker is introduced by weirdologist John Pelan.

Max Afford Novels — *Owl of Darkness, Death's Mannikins, Blood on His Hands, The Dead Are Blind, The Sheep and the Wolves, Sinners in Paradise* and *Two Locked Room Mysteries and a Ripping Yarn* by one of Australia's finest mystery novelists.

Mistress of Terror — Fourth volume of the collected weird tales of Wyatt Blassingame.

Money Brawl — Two books about the writing business by Jack Woodford and H. Bedford-Jones. Introduced by Richard A. Lupoff.

More Secret Adventures of Sherlock Holmes — Gary Lovisi's second collection of tales about the unknown sides of the great detective.

Muddled Mind: Complete Works of Ed Wood, Jr. — David Hayes and Hayden Davis deconstruct the life and works of the mad, but canny, genius.

Murder among the Nudists — A mystery from 1934 by Peter Hunt, featuring a naked Detective-Inspector going undercover in a nudist colony.

Murder in Black and White — 1931 classic tennis whodunit by Evelyn Elder.

Murder in Shawnee — Two novels of the Alleghenies by John Douglas: *Shawnee Alley Fire* and *Haunts*.

Murder in Silk — A 1937 Yellow Peril novel of the silk trade by Ralph Trevor.

Murder in Suffolk — A 1938 murder mystery by mysterious author A. Fielding.

My Deadly Angel — 1955 Cold War drama by John Chelton.

My First Time: The One Experience You Never Forget — Michael Birchwood — 64 true first-person narratives of how they lost it.

My Touch Brings Death — Second volume of collected stories by Russell Gray.

Mysterious Martin, the Master of Murder — Two versions of a strange 1912 novel by Tod Robbins about a man who writes books that can kill.

Norman Berrow Novels — *The Bishop's Sword, Ghost House, Don't Go Out After Dark, Claws of the Cougar, The Smokers of Hashish, The Secret Dancer, Don't Jump Mr. Boland!, The Footprints of Satan, Fingers for Ransom, The Three Tiers of Fantasy, The Spaniard's Thumb, The Eleventh Plague, Words Have Wings, One Thrilling Night, The Lady's in Danger, It Howls at Night, The Terror in the Fog, Oil Under the Window, Murder in the Melody, The Singing Room.* This is the complete Norman Berrow library of locked-room mysteries, several of which are masterpieces.

Old Faithful and Other Stories — SF classic tales by Raymond Z. Gallun

Old Times' Sake — Short stories by James Reasoner from Mike Shayne Magazine.

One Dreadful Night — A classic mystery by Ronald S. L. Harding

Pair O' Jacks — A mystery novel and a diatribe about publishing by Jack Woodford

Perfect .38 — Two early Timothy Dane novels by William Ard. More to come.

Prince Pax — Devilish intrigue by George Sylvester Viereck and Philip Eldridge

Prose Bowl — Futuristic satire of a world where hack writing has replaced football as our national obsession, by Bill Pronzini and Barry N. Malzberg.

Red Light — The history of legal prostitution in Shreveport Louisiana by Eric Brock. Includes wonderful photos of the houses and the ladies.

Researching American-Made Toy Soldiers — A 276-page collection of a lifetime of articles by toy soldier expert Richard O'Brien.

Reunion in Hell — Volume One of the John H. Knox series of weird stories from the pulps. Introduced by horror expert John Pelan.

Ripped from the Headlines! — The Jack the Ripper story as told in the newspaper articles in the *New York* and *London Times*.

Rough Cut & New, Improved Murder — Ed Gorman's first two novels.

R. R. Ryan Novels — *Freak Museum, The Subjugated Beast, Death of a Sadist* and *Echo of a Curse* – introduced by John Pelan.

Ruby of a Thousand Dreams — The villain Wu Fang returns in this Roland Daniel novel.

Ruled By Radio — 1925 futuristic novel by Robert L. Hadfield & Frank E. Farncombe.

Rupert Penny Novels — *Policeman's Holiday, Policeman's Evidence, Lucky Policeman, Policeman in Armour, Sealed Room Murder, Sweet Poison, The Talkative Policeman, She had to Have Gas* and *Cut and Run* (by Martin Tanner.) Rupert Penny is the pseudonym of Australian Charles Thornett, a master of the locked room, impossible crime plot.

Sacred Locomotive Flies — Richard A. Lupoff's psychedelic SF story.

Sam — Early gay novel by Lonnie Coleman.

Sand's Game — Spectacular hard-boiled noir from Ennis Willie, edited by Lynn Myers and Stephen Mertz, with contributions from Max Allan Collins, Bill Crider, Wayne Dundee, Bill Pronzini, Gary Lovisi and James Reasoner.

Sand's War — More violent fiction from the typewriter of Ennis Willie

Satan's Den Exposed — True crime in Truth or Consequences New Mexico — Award-winning journalism by the *Desert Journal*.

Satan's Secret and Selected Stories — Barnard Stacey's only novel with a selection of his best short stories.

Satans of Saturn — Novellas from the pulps by Otis Adelbert Kline and E. H. Price

Satan's Sin House and Other Stories — Horrific gore by Wayne Rogers

Secrets of a Teenage Superhero — Graphic lit by Jonathan Sweet

Sex Slave — Potboiler of lust in the days of Cleopatra by Dion Leclerq, 1966.

Sideslip — 1968 SF masterpiece by Ted White and Dave Van Arnam.

Slammer Days — Two full-length prison memoirs: *Men into Beasts* (1952) by George Sylvester Viereck and *Home Away From Home* (1962) by Jack Woodford.

Slippery Staircase — 1930s whodunit from E.C.R. Lorac

Sorcerer's Chessmen — John Pelan introduces this 1939 classic by Mark Hansom.

Star Griffin — Michael Kurland's 1987 masterpiece of SF drollery is back.

Stakeout on Millennium Drive — Award-winning Indianapolis Noir by Ian Woollen.

Strands of the Web: Short Stories of Harry Stephen Keeler — Edited and Introduced by Fred Cleaver.

Summer Camp for Corpses and Other Stories — Weird Menace tales from Arthur Leo Zagat; introduced by John Pelan.

Suzy — A collection of comic strips by Richard O'Brien and Bob Vojtko from 1970.

Tales of the Macabre and Ordinary — Modern twisted horror by Chris Mikul, author of the *Bizarrism* series.

Tales of Terror and Torment Vols. #1 & #2 — John Pelan selects and introduces these samplers of weird menace tales from the pulps.

Tenebrae — Ernest G. Henham's 1898 horror tale brought back.

The Alice Books — Lewis Carroll's classics *Alice's Adventures in Wonderland* and *Through the Looking-Glass* together in one volume, with new illustrations by O'Keefe.

The Amorous Intrigues & Adventures of Aaron Burr — by Anonymous. Hot historical action about the man who almost became Emperor of Mexico.

The Anthony Boucher Chronicles — edited by Francis M. Nevins. Book reviews by Anthony Boucher written for the *San Francisco Chronicle,* 1942 – 1947. Essential and fascinating reading by the best book reviewer there ever was.

The Barclay Catalogs — Two essential books about toy soldier collecting by Richard O'Brien

The Basil Wells Omnibus — A collection of Wells' stories by Richard A. Lupoff

The Beautiful Dead and Other Stories — Dreadful tales from Donald Dale

The Best of 10-Story Book — edited by Chris Mikul, over 35 stories from the literary magazine Harry Stephen Keeler edited.

The Bitch Wall — Novel about American soldiers in the Vietnam War, based on Dennis Lane's experiences.

The Black Dark Murders — Vintage 50s college murder yarn by Milt Ozaki, writing as Robert O. Saber.

The Book of Time — The classic novel by H.G. Wells is joined by sequels by Wells himself and three stories by Richard A. Lupoff. Illustrated by Gavin L. O'Keefe.

The Broken Fang and Other Experiences of a Specialist in Spooks — Eerie mystery tales by Uel Key.

The Case in the Clinic — One of E.C.R. Lorac's finest.

The Strange Case of the Antlered Man — A mystery of superstition by Edwy Searles Brooks.

The Case of the Bearded Bride — #4 in the Day Keene in the Detective Pulps series.

The Case of the Little Green Men — Mack Reynolds wrote this love song to sci-fi fans back in 1951 and it's now back in print.

The Charlie Chaplin Murder Mystery — A 2004 tribute by noted film scholar, Wes D. Gehring.

The Chinese Jar Mystery — Murder in the manor by John Stephen Strange, 1934.

The Cloudbuilders and Other Stories — SF tales from Colin Kapp.

The Collected Writings — Collection of science fiction stories, memoirs and poetry by Carol Carr. Introduction by Karen Haber.

The Compleat Calhoon — All of Fender Tucker's works: Includes *Totah Six-Pack, Weed, Women and Song* and *Tales from the Tower,* plus a CD of all of his songs.

The Compleat Ova Hamlet — Parodies of SF authors by Richard A. Lupoff. This is a brand new edition with more stories and more illustrations by Trina Robbins.

The Contested Earth and Other SF Stories — A never-before published space opera and seven short stories by Jim Harmon.

The Corpse Factory — More horror stories by Arthur Leo Zagat.

The Crackpot and Other Twisted Tales of Greedy Fans and Collectors — The first retrospective collection of the whacky stories of John E. Stockman. Edited by Dwight R. Decker.

The Crimson Butterfly — Early novel by Edmund Snell involving superstition and aberrant Lepidoptera in Borneo.

The Crimson Query — A 1929 thriller from Arlton Eadie. A perfect way to get introduced.

The Curse of Cantire — Classic 1939 novel of a family curse by Walter S. Masterman.

The Daymakers & **City of the Tiger** — Two volumes of stories taken from the influential British science fiction magazine *Science Fantasy.* Compiled by John Boston & Damien Broderick.

The Devil and the C.I.D. — Odd diabolic mystery by E.C.R. Lorac

The Devil Drives — An odd prison and lost treasure novel from 1932 by Virgil Markham.

The Devil of Pei-Ling — Herbert Asbury's 1929 tale of the occult.

The Devil's Mistress — A 1915 Scottish gothic tale by J. W. Brodie-Innes, a member of Aleister Crowley's Golden Dawn.

The Devil's Nightclub and Other Stories — John Pelan introduces some gruesome tales by Nat Schachner.

The Disentanglers — Episodic intrigue at the turn of last century by Andrew Lang

The Dog Poker Code — A spoof of *The Da Vinci Code* by D. B. Smithee.

The Dumpling — Political murder from 1907 by Coulson Kernahan.

The End of It All and Other Stories — Ed Gorman selected his favorite short stories for this huge collection.

The Evil of Li-Sin — A Gerald Verner double, combining *The Menace of Li-Sin* and *The Vengeance of Li-Sin,* together with an introduction by John Pelan and an afterword and bibliography by Chris Verner.

The Fangs of Suet Pudding — A 1944 novel of the German invasion by Adams Farr

The Finger of Destiny and Other Stories — Edmund Snell's superb collection of weird stories of Borneo.

The Ghost of Gaston Revere — From 1935, a novel of life and beyond by Mark Hansom, introduced by John Pelan.

The Girl in the Dark — A thriller from Roland Daniel

The Gold Star Line — Seaboard adventure from L.T. Reade and Robert Eustace.

The Great Orme Terror — Horror stories by Garnett Radcliffe from the pulps

The Hairbreadth Escapes of Major Mendax — Francis Blake Crofton's 1889 boys' book.

The House That Time Forgot and Other Stories — Insane pulpitude by Robert F. Young

The House of the Vampire — 1907 poetic thriller by George S. Viereck.

The Illustrious Corpse — Murder hijinx from Tiffany Thayer

The Incredible Adventures of Rowland Hern — Intriguing 1928 impossible crimes by Nicholas Olde.

The John Dickson Carr Companion — Comprehensive reference work compiled by James E. Keirans. Indispensable resource for the Carr *aficionado*.

The Julius Caesar Murder Case — A classic 1935 re-telling of the assassination by Wallace Irwin that's much more fun than the Shakespeare version.

The Koky Comics — A collection of all of the 1978-1981 Sunday and daily comic strips by Richard O'Brien and Mort Gerberg, in two volumes.

The Lady of the Terraces — 1925 missing race adventure by E. Charles Vivian.

The Lord of Terror — 1925 mystery with master-criminal, Fantômas.

The Madman — Ingenious thriller by Mark Hansom.

The Man who was Murdered Twice — Intriguing murder mystery by Robert H. Leitfred.

The Melamare Mystery — A classic 1929 Arsene Lupin mystery by Maurice Leblanc

The Man Who Was Secrett — Epic SF stories from John Brunner

The Man Without a Planet — Science fiction tales by Richard Wilson

The N. R. De Mexico Novels — Robert Bragg, the real N.R. de Mexico, presents *Marijuana Girl, Madman on a Drum, Private Chauffeur* in one volume.

The Night Remembers — A 1991 Jack Walsh mystery from Ed Gorman.

The One After Snelling — Kickass modern noir from Richard O'Brien.

The Organ Reader — A huge compilation of just about everything published in the 1971-1972 radical bay-area newspaper, *THE ORGAN*. A coffee table book that points out the shallowness of the coffee table mindset.

The Place of Hairy Death — Collected weird horror tales by Anthony M. Rud.

The Poker Club — Three in one! Ed Gorman's ground-breaking novel, the short story it was based upon, and the screenplay of the film made from it.

The Private Journal & Diary of John H. Surratt — The memoirs of the man who conspired to assassinate President Lincoln.

The Ramble House Mapbacks — Recently revised book by Gavin L. O'Keefe with color pictures of all the Ramble House books with mapbacks.

The Secret Adventures of Sherlock Holmes — Three Sherlockian pastiches by the Brooklyn author/publisher, Gary Lovisi.

The Secret of the Morgue — Frederick G. Eberhard's 1932 mystery involving murder and forensic science with an undercurrent of the malaise that's driven by Prohibition.

The Shadow on the House — Mark Hansom's 1934 masterpiece of horror is introduced by John Pelan.

The Sign of the Scorpion — A 1935 Edmund Snell tale of oriental evil.

The Silent Terror of Chu-Sheng — Yellow Peril suspense novel by Eugene Thomas.

The Singular Problem of the Stygian House-Boat — Two classic tales by John Kendrick Bangs about the denizens of Hades.

The Smiling Corpse — Philip Wylie and Bernard Bergman's odd 1935 novel.

The Sorcery Club — Classic supernatural novel by Elliott O'Donnell.

The Spider: Satan's Murder Machines — A thesis about Iron Man

The Stench of Death: An Odoriferous Omnibus by Jack Moskovitz — Two complete novels and two novellas from 60's sleaze author, Jack Moskovitz.

RAMBLE HOUSE

Fender Tucker, Prop.   Gavin L. O'Keefe, Graphics
www.ramblehouse.com   fender@ramblehouse.com
228-826-1783   10329 Sheephead Drive, Vancleave MS 39565